HE SERVED, WE SERVED

Sheila Melvin

Order this book online at www.trafford.com
or email orders@trafford.com

Most Trafford titles are also available at major online book retailers.

Author Credit: SPC Thomas R. Watkins, Veteran OEF-A

Printed in the United States of America.

ISBN: 978-1-4269-6634-7 (sc)
ISBN: 978-1-4269-6635-4 (hc)
ISBN: 978-1-4269-6636-1 (e)

Library of Congress Control Number: 2011906195

Trafford rev. 04/28/2011

 www.trafford.com

North America & international
toll-free: 1 888 232 4444 (USA & Canada)
phone: 250 383 6864 ♦ fax: 812 355 4082

For my daddy, a Korean War Veteran, who always believed
I could do anything I set my mind to do. Rest peacefully
with the angels and suffer no more. - Bug
Carl E Stengel, Jr
1932-2011.

Infantryman's Creed

I am the Infantry.
I am my country's strength in war,
her deterrent in peace.
I am the heart of the fight—
wherever, whenever.
I carry America's faith and honor
against her enemies.
I am the Queen of Battle.
I am what my country expects me to be—
the best trained soldier in the world.
In the race for victory,
I am swift, determined, and courageous,
armed with a fierce will to win.
Never will I fail my country's trust.
Always I fight on—
through the foe,
to the objective,
to triumph over all.
If necessary, I fight to my death.
By my steadfast courage,
I have won 200 years of freedom.
I yield not—
to weakness,
to hunger,
to cowardice,
to fatigue,
to superior odds,
for I am mentally tough, physically strong,
and morally straight.
I forsake not—
my country,

my mission,
my comrades,
my sacred duty.
I am relentless.
I am always there,
now and forever.

I AM THE INFANTRY!
FOLLOW ME!

Acknowledgements

First and foremost I thank my Heavenly Father for giving me the inspiration and the desire to tell this story in the hopes that it might bring comfort to some, and understanding to others. Secondly, I thank my son for his unselfish service to this country. Without men like him we would not have the freedoms and liberties we have to do just what I am doing now, the freedom to write, speak out and tell the stories of our veterans and their families. Third, my wonderful husband for his service to this country and also for his unrelenting harassment, which gave me the drive I needed to make this book happen. He kept me fired up enough to keep on target and keep writing! OOrah! (Navy). I also thank him for editing my book, as his grammar skills are so much better than mine! Additionally, a very heartfelt "Thank You" goes to the following: Jeckle my dear sister who spent tireless hours editing my book and listening to me rant about this book and this project for months on end. Without her help, advice and encouragement, this project would not have happened. Sharon Corbitt and Cindy Townsend for their unrelenting ability to let me cry on their shoulders and bend their ears and their complete and selfless generosity and support of our troops; especially to Thomas and his unit during their deployment, with care packages and letters and never letting others forget about our soldiers. Jim Carr for his hard work and effort on donating the website he built and managed for our unit so we could communicate with our soldiers and have a way to show them a little piece of home while they were so far away. Sgt. Chadwick for bringing my "boy" back home safe, just like he said he would! Sgt. Jenkins, for being such a good friend and "wing man" as they say in the Air Force; looking out for each other and coming home safe together. Sgt. Robinson, Thomas' best friend, whom I consider to be my second son! Lastly, but definitely not least, a very special thank you to all our veterans who have fought, who are currently fighting and those who will yet fight with devotion for the freedom of God's greatest country, The United States of America; making it possible for us to all sleep safely at night and follow our dreams, and the U.S. ARMY for its dedication in making men out of boys.

*The only thing necessary for the triumph of evil is for
good men to do nothing- Edmund Burke*

HOOAH!
(It's an Army thing)

Introduction

I am the mother of a soldier. An Infantryman. Specialist Thomas Watkins,
A Combat Veteran of Operation Enduring Freedom-Afghanistan. Thomas
is still enlisted, however he is a wounded disabled veteran. He returned
from Afghanistan suffering from severe PTSD and ultimately after his
return home attempted suicide. That will be covered in my next book.
This book will cover his life from birth and take you through his journey
in Afghanistan and his return home. Thomas graduated boot camp from
Fort Benning Georgia and was attached to the 53rd Infantry Brigade,
Delta Company (National Guard) out of Florida in 2002. He was called
to duty during the Hurricane season of 2004 when Florida was attacked
by four hurricanes in one season for the first time in history. In May of
2004 he successfully completed his Anti Armor course. In May of 2005
he completed his sling load inspectors course. That is the same year they
were called to deploy to Afghanistan. He was deployed to Afghanistan in
July of 2005. His unit was attached to the 153rd Calvary Troop and he was
inducted as a distinguished member of the coveted Order of the Gold Spur.
While deployed, Thomas was chosen to serve with the 3rd Special Forces
Group (Airborne) and was awarded a special Certificate of Achievement
for his service during Operation Enduring Freedom in 2006. He also
received a Certificate of Appreciation for Outstanding Service in support
of the 4th Kandak support of OEF Republic of Afghanistan, 1st BDE 209
Corps Joint Task Force Phoenix IV Camp Mike Spann. His unit was also
was awarded a special award for the most successful missions (300) at the
time of separation for the time served.

Needless to say, Thomas endured many encounters of multiple exchanges
of rounds in battle during his tour of duty, including witnessing explosions
of IED's, loss of friends and suicide bombers. I, his mother was in contact
with my son on a nearly daily basis when possible via yahoo chat or phone

when he was not on a mission. This service was tough for him; it was tough for me. But the toll it took on him and the scars it left on him are permanent. I am writing this book to show you who my son is. To show you who all the sons of the Infantry are, and what they do for you. This is just one story in a million. I want you to know my son, how proud of him I am, what he has done for you and me and our country and what all our troops do on a daily basis.

Don't ever take a soldier for granted. When you see a soldier, thank him!

HOOAH!

Contents

CHAPTER I

The Beginning

It is Wednesday, January 13, 1982, 0830 in the morning. I am lying in a cold, isolated room at the Plant City Hospital with an IV running in my arm. I never could understand why these rooms have to be *so* cold! I am attached to a monitor with a belt around my large belly monitoring the movements of my baby, which is now due to come. I am being induced into labor and the nurses are getting me ready as they attach all these wires, and tubes to me. I lay here and wonder if my baby is ok and what he or she is going to be. "Is my doctor here yet?" I ask. The nurses respond and I cannot hear exactly what they said. Hopefully he is here because my last labor was a fast one! Now the moment of truth! The nurse comes in and injects the pitosin (a drug that induces labor) into my IV. It is 0900 am. Again I ask the nurse "Is my doctor here? You must understand, my last labor went very fast and I want to make sure my doctor is here!" The nurse reassures me she will get the doctor here as quickly as possible but she thinks we will have plenty of time.

At 0915 I have my first contraction and it is a pretty good one too! The baby shifts and I know then this baby is going to be coming pretty soon! It is the same thing that my first baby did; I have been here before! "Nurse, please come check, my water has broken and I have to go to the bath room!" The nurse hurries to the room and checks...Honey, you don't have to go to the bathroom, you are going to have this baby!

The next thing I know, I am being rushed from one room to another! I have three nurses rolling my bed from where I am to another room. My doctor rushes in! My legs are put up in these ungodly high stirrups that were made in the 1800's from a torture chamber of some sort and the doctor down between my legs is yelling, "PUSH!" My belly is hurting like I have never hurt before, I feel like I have to crap and I gladly PUSH!

Holy crap, pushing doesn't feel any better! I thought pushing was supposed to make things better! Then the doctor yells "STOP PUSHING". Well now that is easy for him to say! There comes a time in labor when the body seems to just do what it naturally wants to do and pushing is one of them. Once it gets started, it doesn't want to STOP! " "I SAID STOP PUSHING!" the doctor says rather sternly! "I CAN'T!" I scream back at him! Didn't he hear me the first time? Or did I not say it? "Then pant!" Now he wants me to pant, oh yea, now I remember, pant, pant like a dog! Ok, Whoooo, whoooo, whoooo, whoooo, YEOOOWWW. HE CUT ME! "Now you can push" he says. Two more pushes and a cry. I have a baby boy!

It is 10:30 am. He weights 8lbs 11 oz, his head is 13 inches in diameter and his shoulders are 14 inches in width. That is why I had to be cut. The boy is a big boy! But when they lay him on my chest as the doctor sews me up and mother and son make eye contact I can tell you I fall in love with this baby. He is the most beautiful baby I have ever seen. He has such a gentle sweet face and beautiful blue eyes. Something about those eyes, straight from heaven he has just come! He is so alert and wide-awake! I know there was something special about this child, something he is supposed to do in this life but I don't know what that is. I do know that he is special; then he looks at me and we lock eyes for a long moment and I know mother and son bond immediately at that moment with a bond that will never be broken.

His father decides to name him after himself and his grandfather so he is given the name Thomas Ray Watkins. We will call him Tommy. I have only been married to his father for a year now. I thought we had the perfect marriage but as soon as Tommy is born his father begins to change. In fact the night Tommy is born his father leaves the hospital and goes out and gets drunk and does not return. I have to call his mother to come and pick me up from the hospital to take the baby and me home. I am heart broken; no I am in shock! I can not understand what has happened to my loving, doting husband that thought I walked on water. Now here I am, 21 years old, going home with a second child and it seems like déjà vu all over again from my first marriage. What had gone wrong? When he did finally come back, he basically told me I had given him what he had always wanted and he was done with me! No matter, I have a beautiful baby boy and I have a wonderful baby girl waiting for me to bring her brother home and that is exactly what I am going to do!

Christy is so excited when we bring her little brother home! She is my daughter from my previous marriage. She just turned three years old on the 15th of January but she is now the BIG sister! She has been looking forward to this day for a long time! She wanted a little sister but she says a little brother is "ok". She says her brother is her birthday present! She is three going on ten. She is extremely bright and much more advanced than a normal three year old. She also is a big help to me with her brother. She already wants to teach him how to talk! He just looks at her. When we put him on the counter to give him his bath as we remove his diaper to put him in the tub in the sink, he wee's on her and gets her in the face! "Oh mama, he wee wee'd in my face!" "Why did he do that?" I quickly covered the baby with a towel and tried to explain to a three year old about why boys "wee wee" when they get cold! *Sheesh! Motherhood doesn't come with manuals!* I can see right now I am going to have my hands full! I have six weeks off though so I have time to adjust to all of this. I just bought a new house because Tom's credit isn't good enough so we (the children and I) have a nice house to live in. The kids have their own rooms and I have fixed the baby's room up in clowns for a boy. *I was hoping for a boy and I sure am glad it IS a boy but I guess clowns would have worked for a girl too.*

The kids and I are going to be ok. We don't see a lot of Tom. He spends a lot of time with Tommy when he does come home and he dotes on him but he basically ignores Christy and me. When he's not drinking, that is a different story; or if there are other people around then he is a model husband. Me? I have no choice. I made this bed, I have children who need a father and I don't want to be divorced again so I will just have to suck it up and deal with it.

Tom's drinking has become completely out of hand and he spends every weekend gone. As soon as he gets paid on Friday and gets his check he's gone and I don't see him again until Sunday night. Most of the time this is a blessing since it alleviates the fighting which does nothing but upset the children. The only problem is he spends all the money and our bills are not getting paid! The next thing I know Tom comes home and tells me "they are laying people off at work and I think I am going to be one of them. The work is short and they don't have enough to keep everybody busy!" Now I have come to know that you can only believe half of what he says and you have to read between the lines…he's been fired!

Of course I am not one to just leave it like this so I have to confront him and say, "you've been fired haven't you!" Well that did it! His face is now red and he begins to rant and rave like a maniac! He is screaming obscenities that even a sailor would be ashamed of and then out the door he goes! I am now crying and I realize both of the children are crying also. As I lay down on the floor Tommy comes and lays his head on my head and his little hand begins to pat my back as if to say, "it's ok mommy". He is only 7months old and crawling. This is the bond between mother and son.

Christy who is three and a half just says "why do you stay with him"?! My little protector, she is too grown for her age. I have decided I have already been divorced once I am not going to be divorced again. I keep telling myself this and maybe I can convince myself it is the right thing. Heck, I have only been married a year and a half now. That is not a very good record! *What have I gotten myself into this time?*

I have three brothers who live out in Houston, Texas and they have offered Tom a job working as a construction worker with their business. Tom has exhausted all his options here in Lakeland, burned all his bridges so to speak because of his work record. He is a poor option to hire. We cannot make it on just my salary alone especially with a house payment, a new car payment and two small children. My brothers are offering him the job only because of my children and me. This is a very frightening time for me. I have never lived anywhere else as an adult other than here in Lakeland. I have a good job and I have been stable and this means I am going to have to uproot my children, quit my stable job and leave my house. I will either have to sell it or rent it out! We just bought our house and I love it! I will lose our insurance. How will I take care of my children? The resolution is Tom will go out to Texas first, he will go ahead and get started working and find a place for us to live. I will look for work to apply for and put in applications. If I get an interview, then I will go out for the interview before I leave my job! My brother here in Lakeland said he would rent our house by making the payments on the house and the insurance when I move out. This is acceptable to me and takes a load off my mind. I do get an interview with an oil company and had an interview set up. I scheduled some vacation time and all was well or so I thought. *My spider senses started tingling. Something just isn't right. It's just your imagination Sheila. No it isn't! You have been here before! Something is wrong. You have called and called. The brothers won't give you a straight answer. Tom isn't answering the phone. Here we go again. Just wait until your interview and then you can see for yourself!* **No**, *a surprise visit is what you need! Find out now! Don't be a fool again! Don't put your children through this!! The rest of the night was restless and sleep avoided me.*

When I got to work this morning I told my boss I was going to have to take some extra time off. I go in and talked to him about my concerns. Doug and I are friends. He is like my Dad really. He can tell me what to do. "Women always know Sheila, there's no need to go out there, and if you have a feeling then you already know. I haven't figured out how you women do that and I have been married three times!" he tells me. "I have to go anyway, I have to see for myself!" He gives me the time off. I call the grandmothers and get them to keep the children as I do not want them to have to be a part of what I know is coming and that is going to be a hugh confrontation! Not to mention it is going to be a long drive! I left Lakeland on Thursday night around 2100 hrs. It is now Friday 1900 hrs. I have made very good time! I drove straight through. Now I just have to find the apartment that Tom has rented for us and see where it is we supposedly are going to live. I also will see for myself if he has someone there; or if he is even there at all! As far as I know he is out in one of the bars! He is supposed to be saving the money he makes to help us move out here but he cannot manage money at all! I finally find the apartment. It is a nice little apartment at least on the outside in a fairly nice complex; I am actually impressed! But then Tom has very expensive taste and likes to live above his means! *Can we afford this place?* Tom's car is in the parking space. *Spider senses again! Go away! You don't know anything!* I got to the door and knocked. I obviously don't have a key. Tom came to the door. "Hey! What are you doing here?" (Chuckle, chuckle) I hate that stupid little chuckle he gives when I know he is getting ready to lie to me or he is hiding something. His voice is shaky…. *Spider senses….* "Hey I say." "Well come on in. Sit down. You must be tired. Can I get you something to drink?" He's being way too nice! *Spider senses…. go look around the house! You are paranoid…go look around the house anyway!* "Yes something to drink would be great! I think I'll go with you, as I would love to see the whole place! (*Smile*). We act like we are casual acquaintances instead of husband and wife. I am quite sure at this point this is not a surprise visit. He was expecting me. *His mother! His mother had to have called him and let him know I was coming!*

We are in the kitchen now and as he fixes the drinks in the glasses his hands begin to shake a little. "So why are you here?" he asks. "Oh, I just thought I would come out and pick up some job applications. *How lame does that sound? I already have an interview scheduled!"* So show me the rest of the apartment! (Smile). Hesitantly, as if I had asked him to jump off the empire state building, he started showing me the place. He started with the Kitchen where we were standing. It has a few dishes he had purchased and a couple of dishtowels. We then moved to the children's room, which was empty of course since we have not moved anything there. The Living room has a small table and lamp, a lounger and a TV. He has avoided the room, which was supposed to be ours until last. *Spider senses, spider senses....* It has a mattress that lay on the floor, which is ruffled and unmade, everything else in the room is immaculate. Tom is a neat freak so I found it quite odd that the bed is in the condition it is in. The TV is on in the Living room and I know he has been sitting in the living room when I came in. All I had to do was look at him once and I KNEW! I said, "Your mother called and told you I was coming didn't she?" He began to stutter and fumble for his words, and I became furious. That's when I lost it! "Where's your girlfriend Tom? Or your little one nighter, or whatever you want to call her? " I began looking in the closet, I was angry and tossing sheets, throwing a fit would be accurate! Of course he was in complete denial and told me I was crazy. That was his answer to everything I did when I questioned anything he did, I was crazy. That's when I saw it! Tiny, small, shiny, but definitely there! I just stopped. Very carefully I leaned over in the bed and scooped it out of the bed and I handed it to him. "You might want to return this to your girlfriend because it doesn't belong to me!" There it was staring up at him like a hugh heavy rock, burning a hole in his hand was a tiny diamond earring.

A FEW MONTHS LATER

Call me crazy but we did move to Texas. I did get my job at the oil company and all seems to have settled down for now. Tom is working with my brothers and goes to work and he comes home. I get the check on every

Friday for the first time in quite a while. The children are growing and Tommy is walking. He and his sister play together and he is the sweetest baby I have ever seen. He is always happy. He laughs and his laugh is so infectious. He has the biggest blue eyes and dimples and the blondest hair. We call him our little toe head! He will sit for hours by himself and play with his toys with out needing attention. I sit and watch him play and he makes all these noises as he plays with his toys like he is in his own little world. Occasionally he will look up at me and just grin this wide grin with his two little teeth showing and those eyes. *There has always been something about those eyes.* They are gentle and piercing and deep blue, like he can see into your soul. Mother and son lock eyes and again you can feel the bond that holds them together, and then he is back in his little world playing with his toys. There is some mischief in that little boy even as a 1 year old. He will go up to his sister as she sits and watches TV. As he puts his arms around her from behind and hugs her and kisses her on the cheek the other hand reaches up and grabs her ponytail and yanks her to the floor. She is now up and irate and after him as he takes off running, squealing with laughter. This is not the first time he has done this and she falls for it every time. You can't help but laugh but I have to stop him and tell him he can't do that. "I sorry sissy, I'm sorry". Tears well up in his eyes as he hugs his sister. "I sorry." There is genuine hurt in his eyes as you can see he did not mean to hurt his sister. She hugs him and all is well....

My how time flies when you get caught up in the everyday of life...I just got laid off from my job at the oil company but that isn't necessarily a bad thing. I have started night school to become a Medical Assistant. Christy has been really sick, things have been horribly bad with Tom, as his drinking has again gotten out of control and his philandering, well I don't think that is ever going to stop. I have come to the conclusion I am going to have no choice but to try and get out of this marriage. It has now become physical and the children are starting to suffer. Every time Tom wants an excuse to leave, he will come home, start a fight and then leave. This usually occurs every Friday night like clockwork! That will be the last time I will see him for the whole weekend. My nerves are bad, I am unstable and I pitch a fit, throw things around the house, scream and cry before I realize I am affecting the children. Then we all sit down and cry together! If it is a school night, I have to scramble to find a babysitter, try to pull myself together and then go to school and act like all is well and absorb whatever it is the teacher is teaching that particular night! I don't know how much more the kids or me can take of this! I just have to get through school! I have learned to be clever, I know when he has a date, and I don't give him a chance to start the fight. As soon as he walks in, I tell him, "have a good night, I'll be back as soon as school is out! Dinner is on the stove and the kids have already had their baths!" then I quickly **run** out the door and to the car. I can see him at the door seething with anger but I really don't care. I know he won't hurt the kids, it's me he hates, he's told me as much! He is waiting when I get home and he is drunk and he is angry. As I open the door to enter the house I see him holding a hammer in his hand. My heart starts to race and now I am scared. Out of nowhere Tommy comes into the room, "MOMMY"! He races to my arms! Tom is angrier, his face turns red and he looks like he is going to explode as he throws the hammer to the floor and stomps out the door. I have never been so happy to see my son's happy smiling face, as I am right now. He looks into my eyes with his beautiful blue eyes, holds my cheeks with his hands and gives me a big kiss. *Those eyes again. The bond we have, mother and son…*

The days are wonderful! I get to spend them with the kids. I am no longer working during the day and only going to school at night. I am now on unemployment and it will take me through until I graduate school. I only have a few more months to go so I can do this! Tommy is such a joy. For a two year old he is so inquisitive. He has to take everything apart, look at it and then he tries to put it all back together. He does put it back together but it looks absolutely NOTHING like it did before! "Look mommy! I did it" "yes sir you sure did!" he just beams at me with those blue eyes as I say this like he has conquered the world! I think someday he might. I feel sadness in my heart for this beautiful softhearted child even now as I feel like someday in the future he will be taken advantage of because he is so soft hearted. He is such a loving child. He is a happy child. And those beautiful blue eyes, and blonde hair, the girls will be coming out of the woodwork. Oh this mother's heart and the child is only two! Does every mother worry about their children like this so small?

I realize after last night things are overwhelmingly dangerous! Tom has been telling me from time to time he is going to kill me but I really haven't taken it serious. *I can't breath, something is around my neck, I awaken to find Tom on top of me with his hands around my neck! He's chocking me! He's trying to kill me in my sleep! He's drunk I can smell the stench of stale booze on his breath his face is so close to mine. I started kicking, scratching, and fighting for my life! I finally got him off of me! I started screaming at him "get out of here" and he just glared at me. I have never seen eyes so blank, but he staggered out of the room and into the living room. I placed a chair against the doorknob and for the rest of the night there was no sleep for me! The next morning when I was still mad and he claims he had no recollection of the event and he was drunk, as if that gave him a good excuse! But I covered the bruises on my neck and chalked it up to his being drunk…. he didn't mean it.* I realize now maybe he does mean it! He wasn't drunk last night! And what was he doing with that hammer and why did he get so mad when Tommy came in the room and leave? Was he going to hit **me** with it? If he is that unstable are the children in danger? He has never been aggressive or shown any violence toward them. I am going to have to take better measures to protect myself! I will just have to be cleverer than he is! Tom is a coward, he is good at picking on me when no one is around but he acts like he adores me if there is an audience! I can't stand feeling his grimy hands on me anymore. He is the perfect con man. I don't know this man. He is not the man I married. From now on I will bring a friend home to spend the night with me after school! Tom is absolutely furious! I think this just fuels his fire even more. His hatred for me grows.

1-year later- 1984

I got up to go to work today and when I go out to get in my car it is gone! I can't believe it! My Tercel that I have worked so hard to get with my credit before we left Florida! I am going to have to call the doctor's office and let them know I can't make it in, call the police and file a report and try and get in touch with Tom. Tom is now working with a glass installation company and they send him all over the state so there is no telling where he is! I won't be able to get in touch with him until he gets home tonight! *Ok, think…*Call work first! Check. Now, call the police. "I would like to report a stolen car". Give them all the information. What they have to say next makes my heart sink and I think I am going to just puke. "Can you say that again please?" I said. "Yes ma'am, your car was not stolen, it was repossessed this morning at 0600am for lack of payment." "Thank you." I say as I hang up the phone. Tom insisted on paying all the bills and taking care of the finances. He assured me the car payments were being made. *I guess not.* He lies about every thing else I should have know he was lying about that too! I guess this is going to be another big fight tonight and I guess another beating for me. I fight back but I am no match for him. Of course if you ask him he will tell you I beat him up…funny how it's me who always ends up with the black eyes.

"Why didn't you make the car payments?!" I ask, no I scream! His face turns red, then his ears and now here it comes, the loud assertive, I am the man voice. First the stutter, then "I can't pay everything all at once, they told me they would work with me on one payment!" I retorted "it's not one payment Tom, they repossessed the car today! Now I have no car! We have no car! How do you expect me to get to work now? You have your work truck! And oh by the way, where has all the money gone??" *The red face, here it comes!* I scream at the kids to run to my room, which they do! I run to the room and Tommy, Christy and I, barricaded us in the bedroom and put a chair up against the door so Tom can't get in. He keeps saying, "I'm going to kill you!" The children are terrified! Tommy looks up with his beautiful two-year-old blue eyes and says, " I won't let him kill you mommy!" All I can do is hug him as the tears roll down my face. Christy says, "If he tries to kill you mommy I'll just kill him first!" These are my sweet protective children. I hold both of the children until they fall asleep. Tom banged on the door until he was too drunk and finally passed out on the couch. I keep vigil all night; there is no sleep again for me tonight.

4 years later- 1988

Tom and I have been divorced now since 1984. We moved back to Florida and I have been living with a man since 1985. The children have grown so big. Tommy is now six years old and Christy is nine. I am working as a nurse at an Emergency Clinic and also in our Landscaping Business that Rick and I started a couple of years ago. Rick and I fight a lot, I think because we work together so much but mostly because of his drinking. I think also I want to get married and Rick doesn't. He tells me we are going to get married but not right now. I have been hearing this for the last two years. My conscience is now getting to me and my children are asking questions. They call him daddy and they want to know why we aren't married. How do you explain this to a nine year old and a six year old? Christy already knows and she tells me I should just leave. She thinks I am unhappy and she just wants me happy. However she loves Rick, and she has internal conflict so she is becoming angry and unhappy herself! Tommy, well he just looks up with those blue eyes so innocently and your heart melts. All he wants to know is why mommy and daddy aren't married like the other kids parents. The stress is overwhelming to me and it causes fights and I am not a very trusting type at this point either! I don't trust Rick. That causes a lot of tension in this relationship. Because of this I have decided the kids and I need to leave. When I tell Rick this all he says is "go!" He leaves and goes to the bar.

With two garbage bags of clothes, my car and my kids, I end up in Warner Robins, Georgia at 0400. I knock lightly on my dad's door and let myself in. We have been on the road now for seven hours and I am tired! The kids are sound asleep and I lay them on the couch. My stepmom meets me in the living room, "what are you doing here?" "I'll explain in the morning, go back to bed mom, sorry I woke you up." "Ok," and she went back to bed. Although I am tired, I lay and watch my children sleep and tears roll down my cheeks. What kind of example am I setting for them? What kind of life have I given them so far? How are they going to grow up to be normal people with such an unsettled mother and life? I have tried to give them some stabilization of family with each other. The three of us are bonded together closer than mother and children can be. And I have tried to teach them about their Savior to rely on him no matter what. We always have family prayer every morning and every night without fail. We say prayer if we are scared or if we need help. We say prayer if we are sick. Tommy always tells me when I cry, "mommy just say a prayer and you will feel all better!" Christy is always the one who reminds us to have our morning prayer before school! Have I done enough? I say a prayer and fall asleep.

I awake with a little hand on my face and two big blue eyes looking straight into mine, "Mommy! We are at grandpa's!" "We are?" I say. "How did we get here?" I ask. "I don't know mommy! But they have goats and rabbits!" "Come on mommy get up and come look!" He grabs my hand with his sweet little hand and tries to drag me out of bed. I look at those big blue eyes, soft and full of life and excitement! How can I resist. "Ok, ok!" I get up, I am still in my clothes so all I have to do is slip on my shoes and out the door we go. The sun is so bright but there is a chill in the air for September. *We never felt that kind of chill so early in Florida!* Tommy had already taken off ahead of me and sure enough there is a large Billy goat and Tommy butting heads fighting for "king of the hill" at the top of a dirt mound! "Tommy!" "Don't let that goat hit you in the head!" "He's not hurting me mommy, he's playing! His name is Abraham!" He looks up at me with a big grin and then "Abraham" takes his opportunity to butt him off the hill! Down the hill Tommy goes! Laughter and giggling all the way down! *Oh this mother's heart! But he is a boy and I guess that is what boys do and they are having a blast.* It **is** kind of funny when you watch! He laughed, I laughed and back up the hill he went to fight Abraham for top spot on the hill!

"So what are your plans?" my stepmom asks. "I don't know. I really don't have any, I just knew I had to leave so I left." I replied. She just stared at me. *I hate that stare. She always has a way of making me feel uncomfortable.* "Can I stay here for a little while until I can find a job and get on my feet? I want to make a new start, get away from everything and just start over!" I knew they never approved of me living with Rick anyway. For the same reason I have always felt guilty, the last place I wanted to be was back at my parents' house but I have nowhere else to go. "I spoke to my Bishop down in Lakeland before I left and that's kind of why I'm here. I had to make a decision and I made it. I have no place to go in Lakeland, so I just got in the car and started driving and well here I am!" *(Smile)* After what seemed like an eternity of silence, she finally said, "Well you know your brother (who is actually my stepbrother) and his wife are staying here and we really don't have a lot of room but if you want to sleep on the floor or couch I guess you can. There's a little room out back behind the shop (she has an upholstery shop in the garage) you can stay in if you want. We can put a bed in there. Now there's no heat or electricity but we can run a light in there from the shop." "The children can stay in the house?" I ask. "Sure". "That'll be just great! I really appreciate it! We will try to stay out of the way and I will do what ever I can to get a job and move out as soon as possible!" I tell her. "You know Georgia has great benefits for single mothers and you can go file for Medicaid. They will pay you a monthly check and you can get food stamps." "Really?" I say. "That's great! I will go down there tomorrow if you will tell me where to go and then I can pay you and dad some money at least for groceries for what we eat!". "I can take you." She says.

It seems like my children always have to be older than they should be for kids. "Now, we are going to stay here with grandpa and grandma for a little while but you guys are going to have to really be on your very best behavior. And you are going to have to stay out of their way ok? Mommy really needs you to do this for me." They both look at me with serious eyes and shake their heads yes. "Is daddy Richard coming to live with us too?" *There were those big blue eyes looking at me innocently again. But this time there was a furrow in the brow with a worried look in them.* "No honey he isn't" I say. Tears well up in his eyes and my heart starts to break, now tears well up in mine, "awe honey, we are starting a new adventure here, pretty soon you, me and sissy are going to have our own house and it's going to be just us. Remember, it's just us against the world no matter what!" I try to cheer him up. "Then I'll take care of you and sissy?" Those big blue eyes were now determined! "That's right! You will take care of me and sissy." Christy rolled her eyes! I smile inside. We have a big group hug! Christy thumped him on the head and off they go! All is well again for this crisis.

The room behind the garage is about a ten by eight foot space and it is packed with old boxes and stuff that looks like it has been in there for a hundred years. The dust is at least two inches thick and the spider webs, oh gosh the spider webs! Did I tell you how afraid I am of spiders? I am close to having arachnophobia! This is going to be a job just getting it cleared enough to get a small twin mattress in here for me to sleep on! *Ok, I can do this!* I have battled worse; a few little spiders are nothing! *Yea, tell that to my beating heart that is about to explode!* I am so glad the children will be sleeping in the house! Small miracles! I finally get it cleaned up enough to sweep it out and all the spider webs swiped down out of the corners and off the walls. The floors are plywood as well as the walls and the door is a wooden door that doesn't shut very well with gaping gaps on all sides. I didn't realize how cold the nights are up here in Georgia in September! There is no heat but I do have a small little plug in electric heater that helps a little. Mom gives me several blankets but I still sleep in several layers of clothes, three pairs of socks, a toboggan on my head and I am still freezing! I just came from Florida and I don't own a coat so all I have is a sweater type jacket and I have that on too! The parents live in Peach County so the kids will be going to Byron for school even though they technically live in Ft. Valley. I will take them over tomorrow to get them enrolled. Five am will come around early! I don't know how much sleep I am going to get; I am still freezing as I cry myself to sleep....

Bzz, bzz, bzz...I can't figure out that irritating sound but it is driving me absolutely nuts! I am agitated and I am freezing! Bzz, bzz, bzz...my teeth are chattering, I'm freezing...what is that noise?? I open my eyes and I don't quite realize where I am. I know I am cold, and I can still hear that buzzing sound. The alarm clock! I am going to have to stick my arm out from under the cover to turn it off! I quickly do so. *The little shed room.* Time to get up and get the kids ready for school! Now I am going to have to go outside and run to the house in this cold! Dang I didn't know it was so cold up here in Georgia in September! I need a cup of coffee. Yes I know I am LDS but I have been inactive for so long and I am just getting back into the church and coffee and cigarettes are still two of my bad habits! And it is so cold and did I tell you… **I am freezing!** But, mom and dad don't have coffee, so I will have to do without. Forget the cigarette it is too cold to smoke! Ok, get ready, shoes on, RUN to the house!

Warmth! It hits my face as soon as I open the door! Ahhh, I run to the heater and just take it in for a second. The children are already awake and getting ready for school! "Hey mommy!" they both came running over to me at one time. "Are we going to a new school today?" Those innocent little blue eyes look up at me with great excitement! "I don't want to go to a new school! I don't feel good!" this was Christy. She is angry, she doesn't want to be here, she wants to go back home to her friends, her "other" granny and back to here normal routine. She doesn't like change! *So much like her mother!* "We will make an adventure out of it! You will make lots of new friends, better friends." I say. Tommy runs around in circles and squeals, he loves adventures! Christy, she knows what I am doing and she finally says, "Ok mommy." She gives me a hug. With everybody ready for school we load up in the car and prepare to head to school. As soon as we get in the car Christy and Tommy in unison say, "We didn't say family prayer!" I have to stop and of course we have to have family prayer! *My sweet children always seem to keep me in check! I sometimes wonder… Who is the teacher here? The children or me!* ……

Two months later-November
The weather is quite cold now, for us anyway being from Florida! Tommy keeps asking me if it's going to snow! Heck, I keep thinking it's going to snow at this rate. Of course I am seeing other people around here walking around in short sleeved shirts and I think they must be completely out of their minds! It's 59 degrees out there! At 70 degrees and we are cold! But the changes in the trees and the leaves are the most beautiful thing I have ever seen! There is gold and reds, yellow and orange! The falling of the leaves as the wind blows and the evergreens that stand amongst all of them are beyond words! The beauty is something to behold. Something we never see in south Florida! Christy has just gotten out of the hospital, again! She has severe asthma and now they tell me she is borderline cystic fibrosis!

The news is devastating to me! From what I know about this disease is that most people don't live to be much past the age of twenty years old! *This is my child they are talking about.*

During her hospital stay, I am totally a wreck! After speaking with the doctors I sit in the hall of the hospital and just cry for the longest time. I have never felt so alone in all my life. But I cannot let the children know how scared I am and I have to be strong, so I pull myself together and I kiss Christy and tell her I will be back soon. I need to go check on brother. I guess the worry on my face shows through because poor Tommy has this worried look on his face as he asks about his big sister. Everyday I go to the hospital and everyday I come home and he looks up at me with misty blue, innocent eyes and his soft little heart and asks, "Is sissy going to be ok mommy?" It isn't until I reassure him that the doctors are taking very good care of his sissy and she will be home soon that he gives me a skeptical, "ok". Once she comes home the spark returns to his bright blue eyes and I think he feels some since of unity, the three of us are back together again, and the world as far as he is concerned is restored.

I had decided when we left Florida that I was going to change our lives and give them more stability so we have started back to church. Christy, while still in the hospital had taken the discussions from the missionaries and we had set a baptism date for her once she got out of the hospital. My dad is a priesthood holder and will be able to baptize her and we are all excited, as the day grew closer! Tommy and Christy both are getting ready! "I'm getting battized too!" he said. Christy and I just busted out laughing! All of a sudden he just stomps out of the room crying. We have embarrassed him. I had to explain to him the word is "baptize, not battize". " Honey we aren't laughing at **you,** we were laughing because of the way you said the word." "Oh, but I am getting BAPTIZED" he said with emphasis! "Right mommy?" "Well, yes but not until you get a little older, right now this is sissy's day ok?" "OooKay!" The boy is so sweet but he sure has a short fuse and a temper sometimes. Rarely does he pitch fits, he is very laid back most of the time for a six year old but every now and then you will see a flare of a temper. But then, he is so easy to calm back down. I almost never have to raise my voice to him; I only have to talk to him. It has only been lately I have seen this acting out! I am quite sure it is all the upset of uprooting him and changing schools and moving him around, and the illness of his sister that has caused his uneasiness. He has become very protective of his sister and me. He gets very upset if anyone starts raising their voice or stands a little too close to me. I have not seen this from him until recently right before we left Florida.

The baptism came and went and Christy is still recovering from her hospital stay. She is on numerous medications and I have to get up in the middle of the night to make sure she takes her dose on time. Most of the time I just make a fire outside and sit in the dark enjoying the quiet coolness of the night and warmth of the fire until her last medication time before going to my little room behind the shed. I am so exhausted from this same routine, and I still haven't found a job yet! Earlier this week I met the woman who works next door in the auto shop. She has invited me to come to her house to play cards tonight (Friday) with her husband and her boss. She says she lives just right down the road and I can be back home in time to give Chris her meds. This **would** be a nice break in the regular routine and give me something to do to get me "out of the house" so to speak. I go tuck the kids in bed, their regular routine. "Mommy, why do you sleep outside?" asks my inquisitive blue-eyed boy again. " "Well, there isn't enough room in here for everybody, so mommy sleeps in her room outside." "Then can I come sleep out there with you so you won't be alone?" "No honey, it's too cold out there for you!" "Aren't you cold mommy?" *my sweet baby always so worried about others. His heart is so big for a child. And those big blue innocent eyes!* "No honey I have plenty of blankets and mommy is bigger so I have more body heat than you do! That helps to keep mommy warmer!" He had to stop and think about that for a minute. You could see his little brain trying to process it! "Ok" A big kiss, "night mommy, I love you". I take the opportunity to escape and off to my newfound friend's I go…

As I get out of the car, I hesitantly knock on the door. *It's not a date, just a card game.* My friend comes to the door, "Hey girl! I am so glad you made it! Come on in! David and I are getting everything set up and ready! Just make yourself comfortable." As I enter the room I see the most gorgeous man sitting on the other couch I have ever seen! I had to take a double take. *This is **not** her boss.* "Oh, this is Eddie, David's brother," my friend says. "Hi, I'm Sheila", I say as I reach out to shake his hand. The sleeve of his shirt is rolled up a quarter of the way up his arm and you can see the firm defined muscles in his forearm and his nice slender wrist, well-manicured fingers. "Hello, nice to meet you", He says. *His puppy dog brown eyes looked just a little too long and I thought I felt my heart jump!* "So, are you from around here? I don't think I've seen you before." He asks. His voice is soft and smooth and very tailored. His brown eyes are direct as he looks at me waiting for an answer. *Well say something idiot!* "No, I am from Florida, I just moved up here and I am staying at my parent's temporarily." *Not too much detail.* From there it was mostly chitchat, niceties as we waited for my friend's boss to arrive so the card game could start. After about 30 minutes it was apparent he wasn't going to show up so I asked Eddie if he would like to be my partner in cards. We were playing spades that night, and to tell the truth I had never played spades before. But Eddie and I played like we had always played together as partners, knowing each other's every move and we won every hand! My friend and David conceded after about four games and decided they had had enough! "Who wants to go out for breakfast?" David asked. It was still early enough that I would have time to get back before I would have to give Chris her meds so I was in. *Please say you'll go Eddie! What is wrong with you Sheila? You are acting like a foolish schoolgirl!* "Sure, I'll go as long as I can be home by midnight." Eddie says. So off to Waffle house we all go. That was our first "unofficial date!"

I am standing in the kitchen of Eddie's house cooking supper and the kids and he are on the couch watching TV. Christmas is just a few days away. We have set our wedding date for January 27th. He is so good with the kids and they love him. *I can't believe I am going to do this again! We have been together ever since that card game! When we started dating we both decided we wanted to take it slow and not rush into anything. Now a month later we are getting married! I don't know how to explain it. It is something I have never felt before but it was definitely love at first site. We have **everything** in common! We have been spending all our time together. I have prayed and prayed about this and Eddie says he prayed about it. He was not even supposed to have been at David's that night. And the reason that David's boss did not show up, coincidence? I just don't think so! I really believe Heavenly Father sent Eddie to me.* All of a sudden I feel a tug at my skirt, I look down and those big blue eyes are staring up at me, one arm raised and brow furrowed with great concern. "Mommy, why don't I have fur under my arms?" ***what?*** He repeated the question as if I didn't hear him the first time, "mommy, why don't I have fur under my arms?" He waited for an answer. I looked into the living room and Eddie was laughing hysterically. "Well honey, you will get fur under your arms when you get a little bigger." He went running back into the living room screaming, "I will get fur under my arms when I get bigger!" I just looked at Eddie, he continued to laugh, but then when

Tommy went back in his face went very somber and he said, "Oh, ok well I'm glad you are going to get your fur!" Now I am laughing to myself hysterically. Eddie was at it again. He always had a way of messing with the kids and me for that matter and doing it with such a straight face. Funny guy!

It's Christmas Eve, and the children and I are spending it with Eddie and his daughter Tori who is the same age as Christy at his house. Technically, I still live at my parent's house but the kids and I spend a lot of our time at Eddie's and this night is no different. David and his wife and son are here too and I don't think I have ever seen the children have a better Christmas ever! I of course still don't have a job so my friend and Eddie bought all of the gifts my children have. I don't think I have ever felt so humbled or thankful to Heavenly Father for being so kind to us. The big thing this year for girls are the dress up clothes so I made them some dresses and shawls. Eddie and I then went and bought them some high-heeled shoes and big sunglasses. They look so cute and hilarious in them! Tommy of course is into all GI Joe stuff so my friend and I went to the Army Surplus store and bought both the boys all kinds of things from there! A duffle bag, army knife, toboggan, boots, toy gun, etc., everything they need to be a soldier! Tommy is so excited we can't quiet him down, our little chatterbox is chattering tonight!

THE NEW YEAR 1989

Eddie and I married on Jan 27,1989. We sat all the children down and we explained to them that we were now a family and that they are all our children. We do not believe in using the word "step" in our family. We never refer to any of our children as our stepchildren, and they are not allowed to call each other stepsisters or stepbrother they are sisters and brothers. That is how it is in our family. WE ARE A FAMILY! Our family will grow closer together because of this.

Now Eddie does not really have a specific religion he believes in but he does believe in God. He does not go to church but he does not stop the children and I from going to church. In fact, he gets up every Sunday morning and helps me get the children ready and makes sure we get there on time. The only thing he has asked is that I do not push my religion on him or ask him to join any church! The children and I continue to have our family prayers every morning and night and we of course say them with every meal! In the mornings, Eddie is already gone, as he leaves so early for work. In the evening however, at bedtime the kids and I go to the living room to have our family prayer and we usually kneel in a circle on the floor and fold our arms. Each night we rotate who is going to say the prayer because we take turns to give everyone a chance to say the prayer. This helps to teach the children how to pray. We always invite him to join us, and he always declines. He will get up and leave the room immediately as soon as we get ready to pray. Tommy in his innocence looks at me and says, "don't daddy Eddie like to pray?" *Now how do you answer this one?* "Of course he does honey, he just likes to say his own prayers right now. Maybe he will join us later ok?" "Ok mommy, maybe tomorrow!" He is now seven and getting so much smarter! Christy is now ten and they both are so much happier than I have seen them in such a long time! No doubt so am I!

I have always had a very strong faith in Heavenly Father and a very strong testimony. Eddie over a period of time does join us in family prayer and is eventually baptized; after which he receives the priesthood. Today he is going to baptize our son! "Momma! Daddy is going to baptize me right?" Tommy is now eight years old and no longer calls me mommy; he thinks that sounds too much like a baby so he calls me momma. "That's right sweetheart, and you need to hurry up so we can get to church on time so you won't be late!" "Ok!" *He's also a procrastinator like his mother! Wait ' till the very last minute to do everything!* We finally make it to the church both children in tow and Tommy chattering as usual about anything and everything that comes to his mind and believe me; you never know what that is going to be! His little mind is wildly full of imagination!

The baptism is beautiful and I can't tell you how much joy fills my heart to see my husband as he performs such a sacred act upon my son. My dear son is so faithful and innocent in his duty and belief in his Savior. I know this is going to be a saving grace for him later on in his life, I just know it! Love for both of these men/boys and my Heavenly Father right now is just overwhelming as tears flow down my face uncontrollably. I look at Christy and she is crying too! *We have the best family!*

It is hard on Eddie trying to work and me being a stay home mom so I decide to go to work but this meant I am not going to be home with the kids as much. We explain to them this is necessary so we could have a better house and they can go to a better school. We move to Warner Robins and I go to work at the Hospital. I am able to see the kids off to school in the mornings and Eddie am home in time to greet them when they get home from school. Unfortunately this meant I was not going to be able to make my famous homemade biscuits for breakfast everyday! "Momma! I want biscuits for breakfast!" he was angry and pitching a fit as he says this! *That's my little biscuit monster!* I have been making biscuits for him everyday for quite awhile and now he doesn't or won't understand why I can't today! "Tommy, I don't have time for this today and neither do you! Eat your cereal and get to the bus stop so we both won't be late!" "I want biscuits!" *I'm going to pull my hair out!* "I'll make you biscuits for supper ok?" *Long pause* "O Kaay." *Finally! Another crisis solved temporarily!*

Throughout the years in times of strife or illness Eddie would give the children or me a priesthood blessing. Either a father's blessing or in my case a blessing of comfort or strength. In cases of illness we would have another Elder accompany him for a blessing of illness. I have always been taught "The family that prays together, stays together". In our case, this was true and helped to strengthen our family! We had to deal with the ex's and every summer we had to send the kids to them to Florida to spend with the "other" parent. When they would come back, they would be spoiled and out of control, especially Tommy, who as he grew would become more and more contentious. I feel like I am banging my head against a brick wall. Every giant step we made during the year would be completely negated and undone by the end of the summer. By the time he was fifteen, he decided he no longer wanted to live with me because he couldn't get along with me and wanted to go and live with his grandmother in Florida. Against my better judgment I decided to let him go. My heart was absolutely breaking inside and I felt like I was dying but I knew I could not hold him if he really wanted to go. I felt like he would come back home I just didn't know when. I would just have to trust Heavenly Father and trust he would keep my son safe.

CHAPTER 2

The Decision To Serve

It is eight am in the morning and I have just finished a twelve-hour shift at the hospital in Labor and Delivery. It has been a busy night and I am really tired. I have just gotten in my pajama and the phone rings. "Hello?" "Turn on the TV", it's my husband on the phone and his voice is very somber. "What's wrong? What channel?", I ask. "Turn it on CNN, a plane just hit the World Trade Center". "You're kidding me!" "I wouldn't be calling if I was kidding." He says a little annoyed." "Ok, I'll call you back". I turn on the TV and as I watch in horror I see one of the twin towers in New York City burning out of control. The upper floors of the tower have flames coming out of all sides of the building and black smoke hurls toward the sky. The commentators are talking about a plane and how it has crashed into the building and something about it being done on purpose. Just as I am trying to process this I see another plane circle around and fly directly into the other tower! *This can't be happening! Surely that isn't right! What is going on?* For a second or two it seems like the commentators are as dumbfounded as I am and have no words to say. The explosion is enormous and the buildings are burning out of control! All of a sudden I see people step to the ledges of the windows and start jumping from the buildings to their deaths! The horror of this is more than I can take! I can not control my emotions as I cry uncontrollably with great sorrow...

As if this wasn't bad enough, the newscasters begin to report that two other planes are missing! The FAA is grounding all planes and it seems the whole country is paralyzed. The two missing planes are then tracked and one has crashed into the Pentagon! The country has come to a complete halt at that very moment and there is no doubt that we are under attack! Terror strikes the very heart of the American people at least it does me! The damage to Pentagon is massive and death and destruction is all around! Terrorists are assaulting us! The one missing plane is now headed for the White House! The military scramble jets to intercept this last plane but before they can reach it the plane goes down in Pennsylvania.

The news reporters are flashing back and forth to the twin towers and the pentagon and reporting on all the damage, kaos and trying to make sense of what is happening. Then as we are watching the towers burn and getting reports from the firefighters and first responders all of a sudden out of nowhere the whole country watches first the one tower collapse to the ground and then the second one collapse! More than 3000 people are now dead including many rescue workers, firemen, and bystanders.

The world seems to stop and life in the USA will never be quite the same...

The Twin Towers September 11, 2001

I am off work for the next couple of days and I am no longer sleepy. I am glued to the TV and the news. I call Eddie back, "Hey," I said. "Hey." "Do you have a TV there at work?" "Yea, there's one down the hall we're able to go check out." "So I guess you saw the towers? And the people jumping?" *I can barely get this last sentence out, I am now bawling again, almost uncontrollably!* "Yes, I saw." "This is really bad" "Try to get some rest, we'll talk when I get home. I love you." He hung up. I left the TV on, continuing to watch the reruns of the planes hitting the towers, the people jumping, the towers falling, the people running, and I sob uncontrollably until I finally fall asleep…

It seems as if the whole attitude of the country has changed overnight. This horrible tragedy has created a closer cohesion and a patriotic love of our country. The President, George W. Bush has vowed to find the terrorist who has attacked our country and hold them accountable. The man," terrorist" who is taking credit for this attack is named Osama bin Laden. Our country now has so many men and women, from all walks of life who are eager to sign up for military service than ever before! Young and old, it appears the country wants vengeance for this tragedy; blood, an eye for an eye! I have never seen such patriotism, and almost a hatred for revenge in such a long time; if ever in my lifetime!

Thomas, *he no longer lets me call him Tommy, he thinks it sounds too much like a baby!,* is now nineteen years old. He moved back home just a few months ago because he has been in and out of trouble down in Florida and just could not seem to find his place in the world. He is staying with us in an effort to try and straighten out his life. He has fathered a daughter two years ago and through our talks, he realizes he needs to get it together so he can be a better father and better example for her. Since he has come home, the rule is that he had to get a job, which he did and he is now working full time and looking for a place of his own. He is looking to "better" himself so to speak. After 9/11, like all other young American men, he has become so enraged by what has happened; he wants to join the service! He seems more focused and determined and has decided THIS was what he wants to do. He wants to join the Army! He is adamant this will be the way to straighten out his life and do something good for a change. "Mom, I can make a difference for a change! I will be able to take care of my daughter, but I will also be able to go and defend this country and pay back these bastards!" "Thomas! Your language!" *I still haven't gotten used to the street language he uses! And I am trying to correct it when I can without being too much of a nagging mother but we just don't talk like that in our home!* "Sorry mom, but that's just how I feel!", he says anger still boiling in those blue eyes. *The thought of those people jumping from those burning buildings come back to my mind, the collapsing of the twin towers...* "I know son, I feel the same way, " I say softly trying to hold back the tears from the memories. Eddie and I both agree this would be a good choice for him. "Dad, can you take me down to the recruiter's office?"...

The Army recruiter takes his application and run his background check. It appears Thomas has been in some trouble with some traffic violations and minor problems so they have recommended he apply first with the National Guard. So that is exactly what he does. Again, more paperwork and then he has to take the ASVAB test. Now Thomas is very much like his mother, give me an oral exam and I can talk and tell you whatever you want to know. So can my little chatterbox, but you put a piece of paper in front of me and tell me I only have a certain amount of time, well, that is a different story. Thomas came home with his head hanging and saying, "I am never going to get in!" "Why?" I ask. "I have to take the ASVAB TEST! YOU KNOW I DON'T DO GOOD ON TESTS!!" *there's that temper again!* "Hey!" his dad broke in, "lower your voice to your mother! "She just asked a question! Either you want to get in or you don't! The test is no big deal! You have plenty of time to study for it and I can help you with it!" "Ok, Sorry dad. Sorry mom, I'm just nervous". *I knew exactly how he felt and for a second, those blue eyes were five years old again, nervous, pleading and needing reassurance.* "I know son, it's ok. Dad's going to help you, you will do just fine!" "We haven't lied to you yet have we?" "No Ma'am." "Just remember, to say your prayers and let Heavenly Father help you!" I remind him.

Night after night I watch father and son sit at the dinner table after the dishes are cleared, and I am cleaning the Kitchen; studying together, laughing sometimes, frustrations flaring sometimes, but the bond between them growing stronger. I watch them stop to pray for guidance and the smiles as Thomas progresses with each new achievement learned.

Today is the big day! You would think it is the first day of school all over again! "Mom, do you think I'm going to pass this test?" "Yes Thomas for the hundredth time!" *I think he is going to drive me crazy if he asks me again!*

As usual, we started with family prayer and he and dad leave to take him down to the recruiter's office. In a couple of hours the boys come home and as they walk in the door, *my heart sank, I get this terrible feeling in my heart as I look at those drooping blue eyes* "well, did you pass?" *I braced myself*...He started to shake his head no but then I saw a quirky little grin, he never was a good liar to me! *That little...* I pop him in the head! He begins to dance around the room like a little boy! Dad and I just watch like parents watching their little boy who was just learning to walk. He was so happy! I am so very proud of him. This will give him discipline and focus. Something he can be proud of.

I am a very patriotical person and I love this country! The men in my family have always served this country. My great uncle died serving in WWII when his plane went down on his last mission. I take great pride in the fact that my father served in the Air Force in the Korean War, my husband served in the Navy during the Iranian Crisis and now my son is going to serve our country in the Army National Guard- Infantry at this critical time when our country needs him!
I spend hours crocheting him a flag blanket!

President Bush at Ground Zero

CHAPTER 3

BOOT CAMP

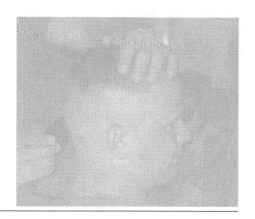

After signing up and getting all the paper work completed, Thomas is now given a date in which he will leave and go to boot camp for training. We live in Georgia and he will be going to Ft. Benning, which is in Columbus, Georgia and we are glad he will be close by. We will be able to see him on days when families are allowed to visit. From this date forward the Army will refer to our son as "our soldier". He now belongs to the government, or Uncle Sam. The families have an orientation time scheduled on the day we take our soldier that will explain what our "soldier" will be going through and what the "rules" are. We are so proud of our son and like most parents or spouses, we hold our heads high and beam with pride for our soldier. We wear our patriotic clothing and pins that show our support for our son as he prepares to leave for boot camp.

Because we are a religious family and Thomas and I have always been very close, we talk a lot about making sure he remembers to keep Heavenly Father in his life even during his training and he will be kept safe. I of course remind him, as a good mother to remember not to forget his prayers at night, and as usual, he just sighs and says, "mom, I am grown, I won't forget my prayers!" We both laugh. I remind him I am still his mother and he will always be my little boy no matter how big or old he gets! Again, we both laugh! He gives me a big hug and says, "I love you Mom". *Tears well up in my eyes, as my son hugs me. I worry that my sweet boy will be going off to boot camp. He's a man; he's my little sweet blue-eyed boy!* "Dad, do you think you can give me a father's blessing before I go?" Of course his dad did and now my son was ready and prepared to go off to boot camp and time for mama to let go!

The drive to Ft. Benning was a long one. We all seem to be in a somber mood! No one is talking too much. Once we reach the gates of the base, we are directed to our parking spot and shuffled to a large auditorium along with all the other parents, spouses and potential soldiers. We are given the "rules" and some paperwork; we are given a few minutes more with our soldiers and then they are gone. We are shuffled out and that's that! We are sent along our way! Needless to say, I cry all the way home!

Eddie and I talk about him every night while he is gone. We pray for his safety. We worry. I worry! *At night sometimes when no one knows I cry and pray to myself.* Not only do I miss my son, but also I hear so much about what goes on in some of the boot camp training I tend to worry the most! There is no contact allowed with the soldiers for the first three weeks they are gone. After three weeks we receive a call and are told there will be a "mid-term leave for some of the soldiers" and Thomas will be receiving a two-day pass! The catch is, he cannot leave the base within a fifty-mile radius. We live about one hundred and fifty miles from the base. That means if we want to see him, we will have to go and rent a hotel room in Columbus and stay for two days! You will have to know my husband and his dry humor, he teases me, "There's no need for us to go see him, and besides, it has only been three weeks! He will be home in another four weeks! Not to mention, no one ever came to see **me** when I was in boot camp!" Well, I can tell you how **that** turned out!

Eddie had entered the U.S. Navy when he was 17 and went to boot camp when he was 18. He only had a father whom he was raised by since his mother had left when he was very young. His father was a very strict and rigid man so he did not support his sons and daughter like most parents would. Eddie left for boot camp with no one to see him off. He was a young man off on his on alone. He grew up fast and hence he became tough and somewhat untouchable. Since he has been in the military nearly all his life, he was much less touchy, feely than I am. I am definitely a touchy feely, huggy person. I cry at movies, commercials, and I baby all my children, thus the conflict in parenting. But we manage to compliment our parenting skills through our faith and living the gospel and through our love for each other. Sometimes I feel so bad for him

(Eddie) and I try to make it up to him, but I won't allow what happened to him, affect how I mother my children!

We **will** go to Columbus, rent a hotel room, pick up our son from the base and stay the weekend so we can spend the time with him! I am aching to see my boy. He has always been my close buddy and I am missing him desperately! Not to mention he is my youngest child and my only son! He and I have always talked nearly every day or at least once a week so this is the longest it has been since we have talked. I am desperate to see how he is, what condition he is in, and I want to know all the details of how he likes where he is! I will **not** take no for an answer! With or without dad I am going! Of course dad is going too! ...

We are ushered on the base and then into a room where we, the parents and spouses, are given another orientation so to speak, as to what our soldiers are and are not allowed to do on their leave time. When they are supposed to return to the base, and there are **NO** exceptions! Then we wait, and wait, ...and wait, and finally our soldier and his company come marching out with the drill sergeant along with three other platoons! We are seated in bleachers and the soldiers are not allowed to leave until the drill sergeants release them. As happenstance has it, and Melvin luck goes, Thomas' platoon is naturally last to be released! I am not a patient person and now I am grumbling under my breath the whole time; my perfectly patient husband has to keep me in line!

My "baby", walks towards me, and I can tell he is different. He walks with his hands perfectly at his sides almost like a robot. When he approaches he is so happy to see us and we are so happy to see him but when I start to hug him he stiffens. N*ot like my normal son. Something has changed. And he is so thin!* He shakes his dad's hand and then all he says is "can we go get something to eat, I really want a hamburger and a coke!" *Now THAT is my Thomas! And he definitely needed some food! He looked like he had been in a refugee camp! He must have lost 30 pounds at least!* His face is drawn in and his clothes are a little large on him. I even tease him, "you look like you've been in a refugee camp!" his blue eyes gaze at mine and we both laughed. "Mom, you worry too much! I've lost a few pounds but I'm getting lean and mean!" he says. "We just don't get all that junk food you get on the outside." He says they are running and working us hard but he is doing just fine. He is just hungry.... *again, my Thomas...We used to call him the* *human garbage disposal at home because he could never get enough to eat and he would eat everything!* The first thing he did when he got in the car is ask if he could have a coke. " Of course you can", I say. He reaches in and took one from the cooler and you would have thought he had received a bar of gold! He holds it up and admires it for a second, then opened it, took a long drink, "Ahhh", he says. The biggest smile comes across his face and for a second we lock eyes. *There was the look in those blue eyes that we always have, mother and son, he smiled, I smiled; nothing had to be said.*

I am worried about him being ok, and say as much with great concern! "I still think you look like you've lost too much weight! And you act like you are starving!" Thomas just rolls his eyes. "Sheila, when are you going to stop babying the boy? He's not a baby anymore! This is boot camp, it's not meant to be easy!" Eddie chimed in for his rescue. "Thank you dad! No offense mom, but I am not a child!" "Fine!" I say and just turn around in my seat! *Men! This is my son! Don't fathers understand that? I don't think he is grasping that! He thinks I am trying to baby him too much and I think he has no caring for our son! We would have to come to an understanding on this point!* "Again he says, "I never had anybody ever even come see me, you are babying him". *ANGER!!! I am so tired of hearing this!* "Well I am so sorry you didn't have family support but our son is going to have our support! We are his parents and that is just how it is!" *That is my solution to coming to an understanding…*Eddie just laughs, so does Thomas, they got my goat! They really enjoy firing me up because they know how I feel about family dedication and family support…sigh! *I smile to myself. I love my boys!*

"Thomas, where do you want to go to eat?" dad asks. He mumbled some restaurant and dad heads that way. When we get to the restaurant, Thomas rushes ahead of me and opens the door for me. He has always been polite like that when it comes to opening doors. *This must be a popular place for the soldiers and cadets; it's full of them.* I thought to myself. Once we were shown to a table and were about to be seated, Thomas rushes around to my chair and adjusts my seat for me like a perfect gentleman! *I about fall off the chair! Is this my son? He has never done that before!* "Thank you!" I say. "That was nice." I smile at him. He smiles back again with those beautiful blue eyes. "They are teaching us to be gentlemen". He says. "Well I like that!" I say. He then waits until his dad is seated until he sits down. Standing at attention with his arms at his sides. I just sit there and I am sure my mouth is open like I am catching flies!

When the waitress comes to the table to take our order all of a sudden without warning Thomas stands up at attention until the waitress tells him he can sit down. It isn't just Thomas, all of the other cadets in the room are doing the same thing! You can hear chairs scooting out and cadets standing up and down like the little pop up guys in the game at Chuck-E-Cheese. It is almost funny to watch after you get over the initial shock! The waitress looks at us and with a big smile and says, "it's ok, it happens all the time with the new cadets! We're used to it!" Then she looks at Thomas and says, "sit down soldier", at which time he sits back down at the table. "We are told we must stand when a woman comes to the table", Thomas stated. *I think I like this Army! At least they are teaching him manners! I like the difference in his attitude I am seeing in my son, and I am filled with pride! I just look at him for a long second before the waitress breaks my thoughts…* "Ma'am what would you like?" she asks. I give her my order. Eddie orders the big breakfast plate. We tell Thomas he can have whatever he wants. He orders a large steak, fries and a large coke. As the waitress approaches our table with our food, Thomas again abruptly stands at attention as she begins to set the food on the table. She looks at him and again says, "Have a seat soldier", at which time he takes a seat. She looks at me and winks. Thomas nearly inhaled his steak and all the food on his plate in a matter of minutes, which seemed like seconds. It was like he hadn't eaten in months! This of course did nothing to ease my mind that he was doing fine. Every time the waitress came to the table Thomas would stand and she would tell him to sit, almost like he was a puppet or a puppy; this had become down right irritating and I says as much. "Why do you keep doing that?! Isn't once enough?" I ask "No ma'am. If we get caught not standing when a woman is at the table by our superiors we will get smoked!" he says. *It is almost hilarious to watch all the boys in the restaurant pop up and down like puppets each time a waitress walks to the table! If you added music to the whole scene you could have a circus act!*

As we leave the restaurant, dad asks, "What next?" "Well if you don't mind dad, I really need to go to Ranger Joe's store. I need to get some supplies." Thomas says. "What kind of supplies?" asks dad? "Well I need some shoe polish and some brass polish. I have to keep my uniform in ship shape. Drill Sgt. is so hard on us and if any little thing is out of order we get smoked." "I keep my uniform the best, I even help some of the other guys with their shoes like you showed me with the spit shine!" he just beams with pride as he says this. *As I look at Eddie I can see the pride in his face and the smile but he will never let it show. He is not good at showing his feelings to the kids.* "Well that's good" Eddie says. "I told you it would be important for you to know, I am glad you paid attention." Off to Ranger Joe's we go.

I am so proud to walk around with my son in his Class A's. He is so handsome and such a gentleman! I have never seen him act this way. I am glad to see the Army has changed him in this way. I was watching my little boy change into a man. He does seem happy; he has funny stories to tell about what his platoon is doing to the other platoons, similar to fraternity rivalries. He likes the physical fitness he is getting. He likes the training he is getting. The Army seems to suit him well. It's like they are deprogrammed him from the old Thomas and are reprogramming a new one! I am pleased with this new polite young man who holds himself tall with pride. I have not seen Thomas hold his head so high and look you in the eye in such a very long time! He has pride in himself and he has self-confidence. My boy is now a man! I can only imagine if they had accomplished this in three weeks what he is going to be like in the eight weeks when he is ready to graduate!

We finished shopping at Ranger Joes and I was tired! I think dad and Thomas are too! " What now?" I asked. "I am tired!" I said. We all decided it is time to go to the hotel and settle down. "Can we get some movies to watch? I haven't seen any movies since I have been here!" Thomas asked. *Thomas always was my movie buff! A good movie and some popcorn…* "Momma, do you want to get some good buttered popcorn and share with me," He asks? *I look up and our eyes connect. There it was again that split second connection; mother and son; quick smile and again, nothing needed to be said.* "You bet I do! That sounds great!" as I smile. We pick up two movies, Saving Private Ryan and We Were Soldiers. We will watch one tonight and one tomorrow. We also can go out and do some shopping tomorrow or site seeing or just hang out at the hotel and visit. Whatever Thomas wants to do. We finally made it to the hotel and got into our PJ's! Dad claimed our bed right away! That left the other one for Thomas. We put the popcorn in the microwave and I let Thomas pick the movie. Saving Private Ryan! Thomas popped in the movie and I climbed into the bed beside him with our bowl of popcorn and the movie started. Dad was on the other bed and before the movie even started good he was sound asleep and snoring! Thomas and I laughing hysterically because it was so loud! "I love you mamma" he said. I just look at him and those big blue eyes. They are serious looking back at me. "I love you too son. And I am very proud of you and what you are doing! I have never been more proud of you! " "Thank you. I am really trying mom" he says. "I know you are son, and you are doing a great job!" He lays his head on my shoulder and before the movie got started well he is sound asleep too. *I sat there for a long time with his head on my shoulder and rubbed his head like I did when he was a small boy. I saw small lines on his face that weren't there before; worry lines. The sun has darkened his skin; his neck was thick and more muscular than I had noticed before, more defined. My little boy has become a man. But in his heart, still had some of his little boy in him. In my heart he was still my little boy!* I finally got up and tucked him into bed like I used to, put the popcorn away and stopped the movie. It would have to wait until another day. I was tired too! I crawled into bed on the opposite side of the bed with Eddie and fell asleep. I awakened several times during the night to the sound of both my husband and my son snoring so loudly that it was hilarious! Between the two of them, it seemed they were pulling the paint off the walls! I could do nothing but laugh. Trying to get back to sleep was almost impossible so I just lay and listened to the, what would normally annoy me, wonderful sound.

The morning came late for all of us! We slept in and we are in just no hurry to get up and do anything. "What do you want to do today" I ask? "I want to go get some breakfast and then I don't care if we do nothing" says dad. " Well, I can go for that, we do have movies to watch" says Thomas. "Why don't we go eat and just come back here and watch movies and spend some time together? I just want to spend time with you and mom!" "That sounds really good to me! " I chime in. "It's settled then, now we just have to decide where we want to eat!" says dad. "Cracker Barrel" Thomas and I both say. We look at each other and laugh. "I like Cracker Barrel" says dad. Off we go. Thomas is dressed in his class A's as they call them and he is so handsome. Needless to say we went through the same routine as we did at the restaurant last night. But we make it through breakfast!

We finally make it back to the hotel and the "chatterbox" as we have always called him was back. He starts telling us about what he was learning. He said his drill Sgt. is one of the toughest if not the toughest one there! But he likes that because it is making him have to work hard and he is learning a lot! He said he has already qualified as sharpshooter and missed Expert by one shot. He is determined he will have Expert before he graduates! *I can see the gleam in his eyes of pride and the way he holds his shoulders high. I am filled with so much pride at this time for my son. Love overwhelms me for this blue-eyed boy.* That is how we spend our Saturday and Saturday night. Kentucky fried for dinner and more movies! Don't forget the popcorn! We laugh, as I watch my husband and my son horse around and it brings great joy to my heart. Family is everything to me.

They say time passes quickly when you are having fun, so I guess we must have be having too much fun. I cannot believe how quickly Sunday morning has arrived! It is up, shower, pack, and prepare to take our son back to the base. With our morning family prayer said, we load the car and head to Ft. Benning to drop off Pvt. Watkins. My heart is heavy but I do not let my son know that! I want him to be uplifted and leave this visit feeling revitalized. I think it would make him homesick if the truth were known. The girls always say Thomas is the "Golden Child", I don't think that is true; he is just the baby and the only boy. He and I have a connection. *He is a little spoiled ok?!*

The drive back home is very somber for Eddie and I. I of course cry a good bit of the way. Eddie remains quiet and just lets me cry. My emotions always get the best of me. I waiver between pride, I worry, and then of course I miss him too. I think as a mother, I still see him as a little boy and I am leaving him at a place where he is playing with guns that have real bullets and they are throwing live grenades! This is a dangerous place and I just left my boy there! Eddie continuously reminds me, "he is not a boy, he is a grown man" "you have got to quit babying him!" I agree with him and tell myself he is right, but then we both know, it is never going to happen! I think, he is old enough to play with guns, he is old enough to play with grenades, he is old enough to die for his country but he isn't even old enough to drink by our laws! Not that I advocate drinking, but what sense did that make? In my eyes he is still a boy! We will just leave it like this unspoken and at a later date we will have this conversation…Again!

We know what his approximate graduation date is supposed to be and are told our soldier will contact us to let us know when and where we should appear for that ceremony. After that, we will have no further contact and the next six weeks will drag on like it is forever. I do believe in the saying that daughters are closer to their fathers and sons are closer to their mothers. I worry constantly. I pray and cry constantly for his safety and this is only boot camp. If he ever does get called to war I think I will probably just go ahead and shoot myself! Thank goodness he is only in the National Guard. As far as I know they take care of things on the home front. Little do I *know!*

I am what you call a workaholic, so I don't follow the news or politics too closely. Eddie watches it every day and he keeps informed with everything and if there is anything that is of any real important then he lets me know about it. If he doesn't mention it, then, I don't worry about it. Now I know knowledge is power and I know I should pay better attention, but I am just so busy that I don't have time to spend on the daily happenings of the news, besides, it really just doesn't affect me! *Or so I think at the time!* Most of the things in the news are about other people. But now, I seem to be paying a little closer attention to everything ever since Thomas in Boot camp. It's really amazing how your perspective changes when things tend to affect you directly. If anything is mentioned about the Military I want to hear about it! Even the National Guard Units are being called up to go to places like Kosovo!

Oh my mother's heart, I pray a little harder every day, not only for my son but also for the sons, fathers, husband, daughters, of all the service men and women. I am beginning to develop a love for all our service people!

CHAPTER 4

Graduation

FINALLY, we get the call to tell us when we are going to go see our son graduate from boot camp. The graduation will take place on a Saturday. The soldiers will have a pass starting on Friday morning again and will report back to base on Friday evening. Thomas sounds so excited on the phone! "Mom! "I told you I was going to make expert marksman! *He sounds so pleased with himself!* "Mom, dad is a veteran right?" "Yes" I say." Well, since he is a veteran, I can either have drill Sgt. pin on my Infantryman's Blue Cord or have someone in my family who is a veteran do it. I would like to have dad pin on my cord! Do you think Dad will do it?" "I think dad will be honored to do it!" I say. "But **you** need to ask him." "I will." He says.

Of course he has called me at work and I am trying to write all this information down, when, where and all the details of graduation instructions. "Mom, I have to hurry up, I can't talk very long, do you have all of it? Are you sure? You know where to go right? Mom are you sure now?" I reassured him I had it all. "Mom, are you **sure**? You are going to be there right? Tell me where you are going to be!" *That's my Thomas, I don't know if he thinks we won't come or if he is just so ready to come home, or both! Sometimes, I also think Thomas thinks I am just someone to talk to, sound off to, but dad is the "smart" one. I am one of his "buds".* We have always had that kind of relationship. I disciplined him of course, but he also has always been able to tell me any and everything. I told him after he got older, I would not judge him, I would listen, I would give advice but I would not abandon him. I may not like what he is doing or his life-style but I would always be his true friend. Eddie and I both have always tried to instill into all our children that principle, that friends come and go but family is all you have! You can always count on family. We have always stuck by that principle.

It will be two more weeks I will have to wait to see my "baby!" Can I wait that long? I am jumping out of my skin. But, what choice do I have? This is going to be the longest two weeks I have ever had up to that point in my life! I keep telling Eddie, "Make sure you put in your leave slip! Don't forget, we are leaving early on that Friday so we can pick Thomas up so we can spend the day with him Friday!" Now, if you really want to hear harassment, Eddie wants to know exactly why we need to go and spend one day with Thomas since we just saw him a few weeks ago and we **are** going to be bringing him home after graduation… I could have killed him on the spot!

Becky who is the mother of Thomas' daughter decides she wants to bring Summer up for the graduation and ride with us over to Columbus. She will be coming up the Thursday night before and then ride over with us on Friday. It will be such a surprise for Thomas to have his daughter at his graduation! It will also be a surprise to have Becky there. He has never gotten over her. Summer is three now and we don't get to see her very often so this will be a wonderful opportunity for papa and me too!

Summer is a daddy's girl and I always hope that Becky and Thomas might get back together. Eddie and I have always liked Becky, they were just so young when Summer came along and unable to take care of her as a married couple. Thomas wanted to get married but he was only fifteen and not old enough to take care of himself, much less a wife and baby. Thomas has asked her again since they were older and she told him yes but then she backed out on him. It tore his heart out. That's when he started getting in trouble. Eddie warned me, "Don't get your hopes up this time; I don't trust her since she backed out once before she will probably do it again." *Darn him he is usually right about these things, but I would still like to think they will get married and be a happy little family. Thomas loves her and he is a devoted man, all he wants is to be loved!* I on the other hand will fall for everything, I try to see the good in everybody; "she seems sincere to me! She **is** coming all the way from Florida to see him isn't she" I retorted! He just shakes his head at me as he walks away.

I have already made reservations ahead of time with the same hotel we stayed at the last time we went to Ft. Benning to see Thomas so we won't have to worry about a place to stay. Becky and Summer have arrived early today (Thursday) and my little ray of sunshine runs to my arms! " Nana!" "Hey sweet pea!" How are you?" "It was a long ride nana!" she says. " I know it was!" "I am going to see my daddy graduate from the Army!" she squeals and claps her hands! Then with the same blue eyes as her daddy she looks up at me and says, "Nana, I miss my daddy." "I know sweet pea but you are going to see him tomorrow!" I say with much enthusiasm. Becky and I then hug and say our hellos and talk for a moment or two. "Where's papa?" Summer breaks in. "He's at work honey." "Is he going to see daddy graduate from the Army?" *I can't believe how much her eyes look like her dad's! It's those same, innocent deep blue, piercing eyes. Something about those eyes! The same connection!* She continues to stare at me until I answer. "Well what do you think silly?" She begins to giggle. "Yes!" we both say at the same time! We both start to laugh! *Her laugh is so infectious you can't help but to smile.*

"Summer, how would you like to go shopping and buy a brand new dress to wear to see your daddy tomorrow" I ask? "Oh yes nana! Please, please!" she begins to run around the room and squeal! "Ok, ok, settle down! We will go!" I say. All of a sudden she runs and grabs me by the legs and gives me the biggest hug. "I love you nana!" We find the cutest little pink skirt and white shirt and pink shoes with white ruffled socks. She gets some pink hair bows to put her hair up in ponytails! Her hair is platinum blonde just like her dads and down her back, long and soft like corn silk.

Friday morning has finally arrived and I am so excited I can hardly keep still. I did not sleep very well last night and I have been awake this morning since about 0300! If I had had it my way, we would have all been up and getting ready then! But, I waited until the alarm went off which was 0530! *Our target was to leave the house by 0800 and that would put us there around 0930 or so.* We finally get everybody in the car and on the way! *It is a good thing I am not driving, I am sure I would probably end up with a speeding ticket!* Summer is in the back seat and just chattering away about any and everything, much like her dad! But the child to be only three years old is very intelligent. She is three going on thirteen! "I think my mom and dad are going to get married" she says. "Summer!" her mother says. I look at Becky and she just blushes. We finally pull into the base gates and park in the designated parking area. We are ushered into a briefing room and given instructions on what our soldiers are allowed to do and when they are due back on base. Now we are sent back out to the bleachers as each platoon is marched out and released by their drill instructor. As soon as Summer sees her daddy she starts to yell "Nana, there's my daddy! Look Nana, it's my daddy" just as loud as she can! The people around us are laughing and talking about how cute she is. Thomas sees her in the stands and is doing every thing he can, not to smile or wave. She continues to yell, "Daddy, daddy, It's me Summer!" Finally the drill instructor releases his platoon.

Thomas comes walking briskly over to where we are standing and without notice Summer leaps from her papa's arms to her daddy's arms! They hold each other in such a big hug and I see a small tear trickle down my son's face as he holds his daughter in his arms. He then gives Becky a big long hug. "Hey pumpkin, would you like to see where daddy has to do his exercises," he asks? "Oh yes daddy! And I want to see the big tanks too!" she says. So off on the tour of the base we go! We look at the bars he does chin lifts on, the running courses, and he starts to teach Summer some of the cadences! We listen as she learns the cadences and they sing them together! We laugh because it is just too cute to see this soldier and this three year old marching and singing cadences. *She definitely is her daddy's girl!* He introduced us to some of his roommates and then of course everybody decides to disperse with their families. The soldiers have to be back on base by 2100hrs tonight so we have only a few hours to spend with him today!

Thomas has already decided he wants to take Summer to the local park down by the river! It's a beautiful day and seems like the perfect place to go! He took me aside, "Mom, I'd like to spend a little time with just me and Becky and Summer if that's ok with you," *those blue eyes looks into mine and I know exactly what he is thinking.* "I think that's fine son, dad and I can enjoy our walk along the river by ourselves. You, Becky and Summer can spend some time together." We smiled at each other and no additional words needed to be said! *Again that mother and son bond!* "Daddy, are you coming?!" He turned and took off chasing his daughter across the grassy park as she squealed with laughter…

The time passes way too quickly and it seems like we just picked up Thomas and now it was time to take him back to the base! We already had dinner, Kentucky Fried, which we took to the hotel room and ate. We visited and talked after we left the park, *(because the mosquitoes here are bigger than flies and will carry you off!)* and the time just flew by! Summer put on her sad face, which did nothing for Thomas' face. The two of them looked like two of a kind! Their faces were identical just one was big and one was little but the eyes were the same. *Something about those eyes and now there is another pair! Even when they look at me!* "Ok! That's enough! We are going to see daddy tomorrow and he will be going home with us, so no more sad faces ok?" I say. "Daddy has to get back or the Army will be really mad at him and we don't want that right?" "Is that right daddy? The Army will be mad at you?" "That's right pumpkin", he says. She jumps up and says, "We need to take daddy back to the Army!" We all chuckled! And **that** was our cue!

Sunday morning came early! Trying to get a three-year-old dressed, pack up all our stuff, and check out of the hotel, then get to the base on time is challenging. We forget to take into account that everybody else in town is headed to the base too! I was becoming extremely antsy because I have no patience! "Just calm down Sheila, we will make it there in plenty of time! All these other people are headed the same place we are!" *My always calm and collect husband! Nothing ever seems to rattle him!* As usual he was right and we arrive at the gate with more than enough time to park and find our seat before the ceremony was ready to begin!

The day is sweltering. The temperature is already reaching into the high 70's and it wasn't even noon yet! The sun is in full bloom and there are no clouds to shade us! As we sit in the bleaches waiting for the ceremony to begin, the sweat is already drenching us and we should have brought a towel to wipe with! *Good thing I put on good deodorant and perfume this morning!* All of a sudden out of nowhere KABOOM! Smoke popped, the bleachers shook and then you hear gunfire. *Your first instinct if you have been around the military very long is to want to take cover!* There is colored smoke everywhere and you can see nothing! Before you know it soldiers are right on top of you; metaphorically of course. The show is dramatic and absolutely phenomenal! These are our sons, fathers, husbands, daughters, mothers and wives! These are our soldiers! Finally the General gives his speech and then he turns the troops over to the individual drill instructors (DI's). They line up with their platoons and march around the stadium for all to see.

Now it is time for the pinning ceremony. The DI's then asked any of the veterans who are planning to pin the soldiers to come forward for the pinning ceremony. As my husband steps forward to pin the Infantryman's Blue Cord on my son, I cannot hold back the tears! This is a once in a lifetime event and I could not have been prouder of either of my guys than that very moment! This will be the crowning moment for me as the wife of a veteran and the mother of a soldier as I watch my husband pin my son with his cord! This is also an honor for my husband to be able to pin his son!

Graduation is over! Thomas has returned home with us. Becky and Summer has come home with us for the weekend and as expected Thomas has proposed. Becky said yes. Thomas traveled back to Florida with Becky and Summer so they could tell her mom and then they were going to return to Georgia, find a place and make plans from there. I have never seen Thomas so happy. Unfortunately as Eddie has predicted, once they got to Florida, Becky did just what he said she would do. She told Thomas she would not marry him. He was caught down there with no way to get home. We had to send him money for a bus ticket and back to Georgia he came. I feel so bad for him! This is about the third or fourth time she has done this to him! He settles down, finds a job, and starts reporting for his guard duty. He is able to buy a car. He now is somewhat self sufficient and feeling better about himself...

CHAPTER 5

Declaration of War- Iraq

Seven Months Later- March 18, 2003

Today has been such a hectic day at work and I decide I will go to the tanning bed after work and just have a little "me" time before I go home. "Hey honey", I say as Eddie answers the phone. "I just want to let you know I am going to be late; I am going to go by the tanning place before I head to the house." "That's great," he says! "Now I can get my nap!," We both laugh. "I'll see you when I get home." I say. We hung up and I head to the tanning spa! *I need that "ten" minutes I get to lay in the bed, listen to the music and feel the heat of the tanning lights and the cool fan blow over my naked body with the smell of the coconut oil! It is so relaxing and reminds me of being at the beach when I lived in Florida! Besides, I need to get a jump on my tan before we open our pool this year!* I finally get into my booth and strip. I am trying a new tanning lotion today and it smells so good. With the fan turned on and my goggles on, I lay down on the bed and close the lid down leaving it cracked a little more than it usually stays. *I never close the lid all the way due to a little claustrophobia, childhood trauma and all that stuff.)* The fan is blowing a nice cool breeze, which accentuates the smell of the new lotion. The heat is warm and soothing on my skin along with the good old rock tunes that are playing on the radio. This is Heaven for a few minutes! I usually fall asleep or at least that place between awake and sleep where I can still hear the radio but my mind is totally clear and there is no stress at all…

Without warning, the music stopped as I hear a special bulletin notice and then the President of the United States begin to speak. I can hardly believe what I am hearing and my head starts to feel dizzy. I know my heart stopped beating for a brief moment! I am now sweating but not from the heat and I have to get out of this dang bed! My chest is hurting and my breathing is labored! *Am I going to have a heart attack? No, no, just a panic attack; I have to get out of here!* I slam the lid open and jump out of the bed my ear glued to what is being said! Here it is, the official declaration of war against Iraq and they are calling up the **National Guard Units**! All of a sudden I realize I am crying uncontrollably, sobbing really and I haven't even put my clothes on yet! *Ok Sheila! Pull it together, get dressed and go home! Eddie will know what to say; he always knows what to say!* I dry my face with the towel, put my clothes on and head home! My body is numb and all I can think about is my son. *My dear sweet blue-eyed boy* Our country has not officially been at war since Vietnam. We've had the Iranian Crisis in '82, which my husband was part of and of course we have participated in other skirmishes like Kosovo and Somalia but we have not been at an officially declared war! *How did the mother's of WWII, The Korean War, and Vietnam handle this? In fact how do the mother's of any of the deployed sons handle this? Am I prepared for this? I have not thought of this, this very moment; when I encouraged my son to join the military. It is one thing to have a husband go, you endure that but this is my* **son**!

I finally arrived home and run into the house. Eddie and Thomas have the TV on and are watching the reports and the reruns of the President's speech! As soon as I see Thomas I could not stop the tears and I clutch him in my arms as I sob! "Mom, It's ok!" he says. "This is what I do! I am a soldier!" "I know, but I am your mother!" I say through my tears. "I can't help but to worry!" he chuckled, "Mom I haven't even been called up yet!" We lock eyes and we both bust out laughing! Eddie hasn't said a word until now, "That's your mom! She's always so sentimental; that's why we love her!" "Ok, I get it!," I say. That's when Thomas said, " I already knew something was happening because they have been stepping up our training. Sgt. said we aren't due for awhile though because they will call Texas and Florida before they call us!" "I'm ready to go!" he said. *The foolishness of youth!* "I'm ready to use the training and I'm going to be the one to find Bin Ladin! I want to make that sucker (*not exactly what he used*) pay for what he's done!" he exclaims! *This is probably the sentiment of every soldier in the Army, but now we are going after Saddam Hussein in Iraq!* "Be careful what you ask for son, war is not all it is cracked up to be. I have known several men who served in Vietnam who said they felt the same way you are talking now but they also said it was much different when they got over there. They also are not the same and never will be! You should never want to go and take another person's life no matter who it is!" I say. "I am a soldier mom, that is what I do, fight and defend this country!" he contends. "I understand that" "Sheila", Eddie breaks in, "just drop it, this is not a conversation you are going to win and it is only going to upset you!" *I am scared for him, but he is a soldier and somehow I am going to have to come to terms with this. I am proud of him! He boldly and proudly stands as he states his case. He is proud to be a soldier! In truth to myself I am praying they don't call his unit! I know this sounds hypocritical but this is **my** son! How many other mothers feel this way? Surely I am not the only one...*

CHAPTER 6

The Wedding of a Soldier

Talk of the war is all you hear! It is all over the news and we are invading Iraq left and right. The different National Guard units are amping up their training and waiting for their turn to be called up to go. This war is not very popular with the other countries but President Bush has declared it as a part of the "War on Terror". We already have troops deployed in Afghanistan looking for Osama bin Ladin and fighting the Taliban, and the President now says Saddam is harboring weapons of mass destruction and helping to fund the Taliban. The Operation Enduring Freedom war in Afghanistan is a multination coalition. This war on Iraq is a war declared just between the U.S. and Iraq! Our military is spread so thin and that is why our National Guard is now being called to go and fight overseas.

Thomas has been dating a girl for the last six months, and today he comes home from work and says, "Mom, I'm getting married!" **What?** *Yesterday I find out he may be going to war and today he says he is getting married?! Did I hear that right?* I am just staring at him with my mouth gaping open. I am speechless and I really don't know what to say. "I think this is the first time, mom, I have ever seen you speechless" he was laughing and his blue eyes were sparkling. "You really got me, I'm going to kill you!", I say, and pop him on the head. "I'm not kidding mom". He says. I look into those beautiful blue eyes and I can see he is serious. I go speechless again! I am washing the dishes when he came in; I just turn around and start washing the dishes again. "So you're not going to talk to me now?" he asks. "I honestly don't know what to say son. You're going to have to give me a little bit of time to process this!" I snap! "You don't have to bite my head off and I'm going to do this whether you like it or not!", he snapped back! "We obviously aren't going to be able to talk about this right now then are we? Maybe when dad gets home!" I slammed a dish down and left the kitchen and went to my room! "Whatever! I should have known not to tell you!" he said! He headed to the bathroom for a shower. The problem is, he knows we think the girl he is seeing is too young for him. He hasn't been seeing her very long and I think this is a rush to judgment on his part. *But then what do I know? I am just his mother…*

During wartime throughout history you hear of several things happening; an increase of babies being conceived and born and an increase of marriages just to name two. Thomas all his life has only wanted one thing and that is to be loved. He is such a sweet and softhearted man and has so much love to give. I am so afraid he is just reacting like many men do, in times like these, evaluating their mortality, and in his case he wants someone who will love him, support him and be here to come home to! *He is so much like his mother! Why did I have to pass that gene to him? The feeling you* **have** *to have someone in your life!*

Eddie finally makes it home! *Thank goodness!* "You will never guess what your son came in and told me today!" I say. "He's having another baby?" Eddie says. "No! But close," I say! "He says he's getting married! I was so shocked I couldn't talk to him! I didn't know what to say!" After a little more conversation we decide to go and talk with Thomas.

"This is what I want to do mom! I am probably going off to war! I want to have a family. I want to have a son. What if I go over there and get killed. I won't ever know what it's like to have a wife and family!" he states adamantly. "That's all fine and good, but I didn't hear you say you love her! Is she pregnant?" "No she is not pregnant! And I do love her mom!" he says. Dad breaks in, "where are you going to live son? How are you going to support a wife when you can hardly support yourself? Besides you barely know this girl!" "She works too, and we can find a small place. I've already made up my mind and I would like to have you both to be there but if not then I guess I will just have it without my parents!" He said. "So when is this wedding supposed to take place and where", I asked? There was silence for a moment, *oh this can't be good, I know my children and I've seen that look,* well we want to get married next month in April and we were thinking maybe here in the backyard in the garden. We just want a really small wedding with just some family and a couple of friends." He looks up. *Those blue eyes staring at me.* "Next month? I exclaim! That's not much time to plan a wedding!" *I'm still in the process of planting my new flowers for the spring! How will I have the garden ready by next month so it is decent enough for a wedding?* "What have you gotten done in preparation for this wedding," I ask? By this time Eddie has left the room. His parting words, "This is between you and your mother! I think it's a bad idea and I don't think it's going to work. I'll let you do what you want, but I want nothing to do with it!" "Dad's pretty mad isn't he," Thomas asked? "He'll get over it. Now back to my original question, what preparations have you done? Do you have a date?" He just looked at me like a deer looking into headlights. "We haven't really done anything, we kinda hoped you would help us with that", he said. "We needed to see if you were going to let us have it here first." "What about her family," I asked? *I already knew the answer to this question. Eddie and I are going to have to pay for another wedding! We have already married off both our daughters and paid for them, which that is what we are supposed to do, Now we are going to have to foot the bill for our son if he is going to have a wedding! Eddie is going to have a cow!* "I don't know mom, you are going to have to talk to Traci" He says. "Well you need to get her over here in the next couple of days so we can talk about it!" *I now have a headache, it is late and I need to get up early for work.* "I need to go to bed now," I say. "I have to get up early!" "Are you still mad mom," he asks? "I'm not mad Thomas, It is just a lot to process and I am a little stressed. Planning a wedding in one month is not much time and I have a feeling dad and I are going to have to pay for most of it! It's difficult when you don't have the money to do much on such short notice! I doubt Traci's family has much to contribute and I still have to make the back gardens decent to host a wedding! That's a lot to do in a month! Not to mention there is a lot you still have to consider, like find a preacher to marry you, get a license, those kinds of things! And, I will have to deal with dad!" I say with some irritation. "Mom you don't have to go out of your way in the yard, it doesn't matter." He states. "It does to me if I am going to have all those people over here! You know how I am! You don't even have a menu, these are things I need to get with Traci to talk about!" "Mom, I am sure whatever you decide will be okay, we will not be choosy and appreciate your help!" he says. "I have to go to bed!" I kiss him goodnight and go to my room. Eddie? He wants nothing to do with it! He handed me the wallet, so to speak, and says, "I don't want to know". As far as he is concerned the marriage is a bad idea and anyway…

"It's the brides family that should be paying not us", he says. "I won't say anything else about it. You just tell me where I am supposed to be and I will show up." And that was that!

And so the preparations begin! Thomas and Traci decide on a date and then pick out their colors; red, white and blue! It will be a true patriotical wedding. Thomas and the groomsmen will all be in uniform. It will be a rather small quaint wedding with only the maid of honor and one other bridesmaid for Traci. They will go and obtain the blood test and apply for their marriage license this week. Traci and her aunt have already been looking at wedding dresses and she has found one she just absolutely loves! She has also arranged to have her bouquet made. *She has been a busy little bee already! That's encouraging!* The bridesmaids will provide for their dresses. I still have to come up with a menu, decorations and figure out how I am going to make my gardens look presentable enough so it didn't look too much like a little redneck wedding! I want this to be somewhat classy for my son but he surely hasn't given me much time to prepare! There also is the object of money! We aren't poor, but we aren't rich either and we are not prepared to have to pay for another wedding! Besides, isn't he the guy? I thought when my last daughter was married; I was through paying for weddings! So this has caught us a little off guard. But I also know if we don't put this together, there won't be a wedding so to speak, and Thomas is probably just as bad as the girls. He has always wanted a nice little wedding with the bride walking down the "aisle", a reception to follow and pictures. *He has always been the sentimental type, a romantic!* I am going to have to make this work! I soon became the wedding planner, the decorator, the caterer and mother of the groom! *I also was about to have a nervous breakdown!*

The day of the wedding! As usual, like any major event there are a few glitches here and there but for the most part it goes smoothly! By the end of this day I am completely exhausted mentally and physically. I have just married off my last child! I am feeling a little melancholic. Eddie? He's jumping for joy! The difference between mothers and fathers …

CHAPTER 7

Hurricane Season

After the marriage, Traci and Thomas decide to move to Florida as Thomas heard the National Guard Unit down there is going to be called to Iraq soon and he wants to transfer to that unit. He is anxious to go full time duty and he is anxious to serve in the war. He feels like this is his call. So off to Florida they go! The unit he is assigned to has already been deployed so he will not be going to Iraq! Me? I am relieved! *Here I go sounding so hypocritical again! But my motherly instinct just cannot help it!* He is assigned to the 53rd Infantry Bde Company D "Nasty Dogs". I had just gotten used to him being part of the 48th Bde here in Georgia so now I am having to learn a whole new set of letters and numbers!

Thomas is disappointed he has missed the Iraq call however, he is attached to the D Company and they are preparing to possibly be called to Afghanistan; Operation Enduring Freedom the forgotten war it seems since Iraq started. There is so much focus on Iraq nobody talks too much about our guys over in Afghanistan anymore! Hopefully this will not happen for awhile! *There I go again! Hypocrite! I just want to protect my son!* But they are training quite hard and preparing for the call. It wasn't long after he left Georgia that the 48th Brigade got the call to Iraq! I wasn't happy when he decided to go to Florida, now I was thanking the Lord that he had! Again, I was feeling a little guilty and quite like a hypocrite. There are so many other sons and daughters, fathers and mothers serving. *It sometimes is easy to forget that others must feel the same way I am feeling now, and yet the call comes and the soldiers go. That is their job! I will be proud to have my son serve but I also don't know how I am going to endure this! Oh this mother's heart!*

Hurricane season is in full swing and there are already severeal hurricanes that have hit the U. S. in other areas. Bonnie was a tropical storm that had hit the state up near Jacksonville and moved on up in the Carolina's. Now there is the warning that Hurricane Charley is on the way and is expected to hit landfall just below Lakeland where Thomas and Traci live. Charley is already classified as a category 2 storm and strengthening. Thomas calls me at least every other day or so, just to talk. We are close, we are buddies. I can't explain the bond. Is he a mama's boy? Not really, it is more like a friendship as well as a mother son relationship. I have this with all my children but Thomas and I just seem to talk and share what is going on in our lives. He sometimes asks for guidance but other times he just vents. Me, I do the same, vent and he listens. When the phone rang today, he told me about the hurricane, which I was following anyway since it is a natural thing for me. After living in Florida all my life, I just naturally follow them during this time of year. "Mom, I think I should send Traci back up there to stay for awhile. We are being called up and will be staying at the armory until the hurricane passes and we are expecting a pretty close hit!" I asked him where she was going to stay. "Well, she wants to go stay with her grandparents and you know we have her brother here too!" *I had forgotten about Richard being with them. He is Traci's younger brother and they have been taking care of him. He is in his teens and a handful!* " So is Richard coming back too," I ask? "yes ma'am, he will be leaving with her. I just don't know how long I will be gong since we will have to stay at the armory and I don't want to have to worry about them!" *He always worries so much!* Traci and Richard leave and come back up to Georgia, Thomas heads for the Armory and Hurricane Charlie heads for Florida!

(Charley-August 13)

On August 13, Hurricane Charley unexpectedly underwent rapid strengthening, jumping from a Category 2 to a powerful Category 4 storm in a few hours, while at the same time taking a sharp turn to the northeast. Charley makes landfall as a Category 4 hurricane near Punta Gorda, Florida. Although the storm causes serious damage, much of this is limited to a narrow swath associated with the hurricane's eye wall. Charley is a very fast-moving, compact storm, and so much of its damage is attributed to high winds rather than heavy rain. Charley remains a hurricane across the entire Florida peninsula and passes through Orlando and near Daytona Beach. (Wilkipedia, free encyclopedia)

Charley causes extensive devistation in it's path and the Guard is busy with it's rescue effort. As expected, there is a lot of kaos and power outages, along with injuries with the cleanup effort. So many times people get careless with chainsaws and powertools in times like these and you get injures related to the aftermath not necessisarily caused directly from the hurricane and then of course you have the looters! Thomas and guard is busy! Traci remains in Georgia.

(Frances-September 4)

Florida is still trying to recover from Hurricane Charley when the next round comes. This year's hurricane season is a very active season and the state of Florida has not been hit more than once in one year in many years. This year is going to prove to be a year in history. It has only been a few weeks since Charley hit when Frances is headed for the state and everybody is preparing again for another hit.

Frances moves slowly, as it crosses the warm Gulf Stream between the Bahamas and Florida, leading to the concern that it could restrengthen. However, Frances remains stable at Category 2 intensity with 105 miles per hour (169 km/h) maximum sustained winds while it batters the east coast of Florida between Fort Pierce and West Palm Beach for much of September 4. At 11 p.m., the western edge of Frances' eyewall begins moving onshore. Because of Frances' large eye, and its slow forward motion, the center of circulation remains offshore for several more hours. At 1 a.m. EDT on September 5 the center of the broad eye of Frances makes landfall along the Florida coast, at the southern end of Hutchinson Island, near Sewall's Point, Jensen Beach and Port Salerno, Florida. Late on September 5, Frances picks up speed due to a strengthening high pressure system to its north and crosses the Florida Peninsula, emerging over the Gulf of Mexico near Tampa as a tropical storm. After a short trip over the Gulf of Mexico, Frances makes a second landfall near St. Marks, Florida.

As far a I know this is the first time a hurricane has hit the same state twice! There is massaive damage both from the rain and wind, there is death and destruction. Again the Guard is called to duty or I should say they are on continued duty as they have not yet been released from their previous duty from Charley.

Traci remains in GA. Thomas remains on duty and their marriage, is already getting a test of what it is going to be like for the life a of a soldier. I spoke with Traci before she married Thomas and tried to tell her about what it took to be a military wife. She said she understood, but when you are young, words are one thing, actually undergoing it and being young, tends to bear another story. At the time, though for all we know all is well.

I hear from Thomas often, and he lets me know he is safe. *As always, the good son, don't let mama worry!* We are buddies, he can share the stories of what he is going through. When it comes rescue, things are exciting to him and it is rewarding when he is able to help someone; but then when it changes to recovery and he is having to look for bodies instead of living persons, he talkes to me about his feelings.

Being a nurse, I have seen many dead bodies. I have seen bodies that have been brought to the morge that have been out in the weather for days, or in the water or shot. I have worked the ER for several years so I was used to seeing injuries and can relate when he finds people who have injured themselves by doing stupid things trying to clean up ! "Mom, today we found this guy who was using a chain saw to cut up a tree that had fallen in his yard. His chain saw slipped and it cut him almost in half through his abdomen. When we found him, I had to help hold in his guts until we could get the medics and the ambulance to him. Mom, I don't think he's going to make it, but he kept asking me if he was going to be alright! I told him he was going to be just fine!" *I could tell by the sound of his voice he was shaken* "Son, you did the right thing", I tell him. "You did all you could and you were there to comfort him!" This seems to help him through his day. I am glad I can be there to help him and glad he feels he can call me to talk. I am thankful for our relationship and thank my Heavenly Father everyday that my son feels comfortable enough to call me to confide in. I continue to pray for him daily. I remind him to pray for guidance and help. It will help him with his choices and his duty. *My heart aches for this soft hearted young man who is now having to see a taste of what it is going to be like in war and he has no clue!*

(Ivan September 20)

The Florida National Guard is now tired and still on duty. They are already depolyed to the Pensacola area waiting for Ivan to hit. I get a call from Thomas on September 20th right as the storm hits the coast and I can hear the wind howling.

Thomas states they are hunkered down in their humvees and will be waiting the storm out. He thinks it is pretty "cool" he and the guys are watching the storm come in and seeing the stuff blowing all around. He says they have to get back in the Humvee to keep from getting hit from flying objects. *Here I go again, worry, worry worry. What does he say?* "Don't worry mom, we are the bad asses, nothing can hurt us!" *Ah, the youth and the belief of how they are going to live forever!*

On September 20th there is heavy damage as Ivan makes landfall on the U.S. coastline in Pensacola, Pensacola Beach, dwellings situated far inland, as much as 20 miles from the Gulf coast, along the shorelines of Escambia Bay, East Bay, Blackwater Bay, and Ward Basin in Escambia County and Santa Rosa County, and Fort Walton Beach, Florida on the eastern side of the storm. The area just west of Pensacola, including the community of Warrington (which includes Pensacola NAS), Perdido Key, and Innerarity Point, take the brunt of the storm. Some of the subdivisions in this part of the county are completely destroyed. Shattering windows from gusts and flying projectiles experienced throughout the night of the storm are common. In Pensacola, the Interstate 10 bridge across Escambia Bay is heavily damaged, with as much as a quarter-mile of the bridge collapsing into the bay. The causeway that carries U.S. Highway 90 across the northern part of the same bay is also heavily damaged. Virtually all of Perdido Key, an area on the outskirts of Pensacola that bore the brunt of Ivan's winds and rain, is essentially leveled. High surf and wind brought extensive damage to Innerarity Point.

(Jeanne- September 25)

At this point over the last three weeks, Florida and the Florida National Guard have taken and beating. And it isn't over yet! There is one more round to go and this one is going to be a punch. Hurricane Jeanne is on the way and she is not playing. Florida has never been hit by four hurricanes in one year ever and this year they are about to make history.

On September 25 Jeanne makes landfall on Hutchinson Island, just east of Sewall's Point, Florida, Stuart, Florida and Port Saint Lucie, Florida, at Category 3 strength. This is the same place Hurricane Frances struck Florida three weeks earlier. Jeanne is the first major (Category 3 or higher) storm to make landfall on the East coast between Palm Beach, Florida and the mouth of the Savannah River since 1899.

Jeanne's track continued to follow within 20 miles of that of Frances until it reaches Pasco County. The cyclone then swings more rapidly to the north, and the center remains over land all the way to the Georgia state line

Preparations in Central Florida are rushed and sudden, as it does not become apparent that the storm will make a direct hit until the morning of the 23rd. It has appeared the storm would pass safely offshore just the night before. Voluntary evacuations were advised on Thursday. Friday, plans for opening shelters on Saturday were distributed to the public, and Florida Power and Light warned that power could be out "for an extended period of time". Canals are also drained on the same day.

On Friday, the Palm Beach Zoo prepares for the storm by moving small animals and birds into buildings such as restrooms and restaurants. Evacuations begin in earnest, with many residents leaving for the Keys, noting that the islands were the only location definitely out of harm's way. For once, evacuation *to* the Keys made sense.

The center of Jeanne's eye achieved landfall near Stuart, at virtually the identical spot that Frances had come ashore three weeks earlier, the first time in record keeping that a hurricane makes landfall in the same place as a previous storm of the same season. Maximum winds at the time of landfall are estimated to be near 120 m.p.h.

Needless to say, the Floridians are reeling in mayhem and tragedy and the National Guard is tired and busy! The Guard will be deployed for at least another few weeks maybe months before they can even get back to their own homes to see what kind of damage is done to their property or if it is even still standing! Most of the guys are from the area where Jeanne had just come through and she had been vicious!

Thomas is extremely worried about his house. He is worried about his wife who is still in Georgia and needless to say he is missing her! The phone rings, "Mom, have you heard from Traci," he asks? "No son, she doesn't call **me!** Have you not heard from her?" "No, I call her grandmother's and they keep telling me she isn't there!" *I can hear the agitation and maybe even a hint of panic in his voice.* "Well I am sure she is okay," I say. "Maybe she is out with some girlfriends or just not at home when you call." *Silence...* "Mom, I think she is seeing somebody." "I think you are just tired son, and I think you need to focus on your job at hand. I am sure she will call you. Maybe she isn't getting the messages!" *I try to be optimistic, but I don't think this reassures him very much!* "I know her grandma, she gives her the messages mom, so where is she?" he says again, obviously more agitated! "I don't know son, all I know is there is nothing you can do about it right now. You have a job to do and you need to focus on that job! You cannot control what she does at this very moment. Understand?" After a few days Traci did call him back. Thomas tried to convince her to go home (back to Florida) to check on their house. He is still deployed in the Pensacola area and will not be able to go home for a while longer. Traci however said she thought she was just going to stay in Georgia, her reason? She told Thomas she is afraid of the hurricanes and she does not want to go back to Florida. She then dropped a bomb. She informed Thomas she is pregnant. Her other reason for not wanting to go back to Florida! She is not going to go back to a house that is "messed up". She is also tired of him being gone! *Ahhh, now we are getting somewhere!*

The next bomb, she has started seeing an old boyfriend of hers! However she assures Thomas the baby is his! *I however am not so sure.* This is devastating to him! " I just knew it mom! I think I should just go up there and beat his..." "Just keep it together son", I have to explain to him this was not the first time a young wife could not handle being married to a military man.

CHAPTER 8

The Birth of a Son and A Call to War

Florida undoubtedly takes a beating in the year of 2004 and is reeling from disaster. The damage is astronomical both monetarily and emotionally. Thousands of people are still without power and still trying to rebuild their homes. Of course insurance is slow in their payments so people are doing the best they can to clean up and make the best they can with what is left of their homes. The National Guard is still trying to help both with rescue of many who are still trapped from the flooding and of course the recovery of the missing.

After four hurricanes in less than two months the 53rd is tired and also worried about their own families. Then comes the call they have all been expecting. The 53rd is being called up to Afghanistan!

Christmas is coming. They will be able to spend this Christmas with their families. They need to get their affairs in order and be prepared to deploy to Mississippi in March where they will do an intensive train up and then they will deploy from Mississippi to Afghanistan. No definitive dates are given and from this time forward we will not know specific dates due to safety issues for the troops. We will know approximate time frames and that will be it! Needless to say I cry. Thomas who has been so eager before is now solemn.

Thomas has always been a very sensitive soul and I am very worried about what this is going to do to him. I know he is tough. I know he is a very good soldier. But I am worried about what is going to happen when he is faced with the actual time when he is going to have to take the life of another. *He can't even stand to see an insect injured.* He talks tough to others but I know him. We will have many talks before he leaves.

His child is due in a couple of months and his wife has not returned home. He is still living in Florida and having to get ready for his call. His wife has moved in with her new boyfriend and she tells Thomas she does not want him to be with her when their baby is born because her boyfriend is going to be there. *Another reason I am not convinced the baby is his! What wife does not want the father of the baby there?!* She will not even tell him what the due date is. She won't even tell us (Eddie and I) when the due date is! "Mom, I don't know what to do! I don't even know when she is supposed to go into labor and she is going to have Mike there instead of me for the birth of **my** son!" Thomas is beside himself. He is almost on the brink of rage! He is about to go to war, he is about to have a new baby and he is afraid he isn't even going to have the opportunity to see his child before he leaves. "Have you thought that maybe the baby isn't really yours," I asked? *I just blurted this out! Maybe it isn't the right thing to do, but I too have been seething over this situation and the head games!* "It's MY BABY! MOM," He screams! "Okay, okay. I am just saying. I just don't understand the reason she won't let you be here!" I try to stay calm. "Because I have already threatened to kill Mike when they came to get her stuff! He's afraid of me," he states emphatically! *I did not know about this! I didn't even know she had gone down to get her stuff!*

Thomas calls almost every day and I try to reassure him things will be fine. I remind him to read his scriptures, and let the Savior guide him on what to do. He is becoming so angry and I am not sure I like where his anger is taking him! However, I certainly can understand it! I do know he needs to focus on his job at hand and things will work themselves out, they always do. *This does nothing to help his broken heart or heal the hurt! Momma can't fix this one!*

Thomas is a nervous wreck and I can hardly blame him. He is preparing to go to war. He is preparing out wills and final arrangements for the "just in case" scenarios. He has just returned from a three-month mission here in his home state that looks like a war zone and is extremely fatigued. And now his wife has left him for another guy, having his child, which he will not be allowed to be present for! I know we are asked to with stand trials and I know we learn from our trials, but it sure does hurt more when we have to watch our children suffer through these difficult trials of life and especially the ones that pull and tear their heart strings! *And this boy has some very tender heartstrings that have been broken and stretched already!* I try to tell him that it is better for him to find out now than to get a "dear John" letter once he is over seas. At least this way, he can get his anger out and get his head back in the game and focus on his mission at hand. Maybe even the anger would help him focus to get him back home. In any case he needs not to be distracted because he needs to come back home and NOT in a body bag! He now is going to have two children who are going to need him! *I know this does nothing to stop the pain that is breaking his heart at the time but I do believe all things happen for a reason. I know that Heavenly Father has a plan but how am I going to convince my son who was hurting so intensely of this?*

I am grateful for the teachings of the gospel that bind our family together and help us to know what is right. By following the inspiration of the spirit we can guide our children and comfort them in times of trials and pain. We can teach them to listen to the spirit and follow the teachings of Christ to keep them safe in their daily lives and Thomas is going to need that now! Both Eddie and I talk with him on many occasions during the next few weeks and encourage him to read his scriptures to find peace and courage to go through this test that is being placed upon him. Christmas is coming and this is a good time of year to just let most of the stress roll off and get back remembering why we are here and what is important in this life. Thomas will be home and I will have all three children home. This to me will be the best gift I could have! We will just enjoy some good family time together.

Christmas arrives and we all discuss Thomas leaving and where he is going and what his job is going to be. His sisters are worried about him but they are also very proud of him. His dad tells him to make him proud and make sure to keep his head down. I cry. We laugh too and I watch them goof around and play almost like they did when they were little. It is a cherished time for us all!

Later, as things quiet down, Thomas and I have some alone time and like we always do, we go outside and sit on the swing and talk. Thomas asks me, "mom, what is going to happen to my soul if I have to kill somebody?" I began to explain to him that the rules of war are different. "Son, Killing during the time of war and killing just for the sake of killing are two different things. If you read your scriptures, it is filled with many wars, God instructed the righteous to fight and even kill for the benefit of others. You are instructed to defend your country, family and land. As long as it is not done with malice you will be fine." He still worries about his soul...*I still worry about him. His soft heart is going to change and I am afraid of that. War changes people; I have seen it before. I just hope he will be able to survive that change!* I just keep telling him..."you do whatever you have to do to survive! You do whatever you have to do to come home alive! Do you understand me?" "Yes ma'am".

The Birth of a Son

Christmas passed so quickly, and it seemed January came and went. Traci would call occasionally to let us know how she was doing but she still would not tell us exactly when her due date was. Eddie and I would talk and I honestly was having problems with this pregnancy. I feel like she is leading Thomas on telling him the baby is his. Yet she won't tell us or him when the baby was due, she won't let him be with her for the birth and yet her boyfriend was going to attend the birth. I just find this a little odd. I am convinced this baby is not Thomas' baby! Thomas assures me it is his baby. He says he knew she was pregnant before she left for Georgia. But I just don't believe it. I feel like he is trying to assure himself because he knows this is a boy since she sent him a copy of the sonogram and he wants a son so badly. I feel like she just wants him to pay. But then again, I am not a trusting person anyway and this IS my little boy she is playing with! I am NOT very happy with her at this time either.

Kevin Wayne Watkins is born on February 11, 2005. We don't find out about this until 2 weeks after the fact. Traci calls me and tells me I am a grandmother again. We already have four granddaughters, including Summer, Thomas' daughter who is our first grandchild. Summer is five years old. Thomas comes up to Georgia to see the baby and brings him over to see us. I really do not want to see the child, as I still am not convinced he is Thomas' baby and in fact I am hoping he isn't. *I have never been so hard hearted toward any child. But if I see this baby, I will be hooked!*

Thomas brought the baby over anyway for " papa" and I see. Papa was the first to hold him and he is really a sucker for babies. *I really don't see any resemblances to Thomas. In fact I thought he had "fish lips" that became an inside joke later on that I came to regret!* Then the baby looks up and our eyes connect and he grins, I was hooked. *Those eyes blue and round... I have seen those eyes before!* He is a cute little baby. I love babies and so does papa! Thomas is ecstatic! So much so he has already gone and had both Kevin and Summer's names tattooed on his chest! The proud dad and he loves this boy! I guess we have another grandbaby, a grandson!

Thomas has Summer with him on this visit so I decide this is the perfect time to give Thomas a going away party! It will be the last time he will be home for a very long time and it is perfect with both of his children here. I call Eddie's sister as she is so good at putting together family parties and we only have a day to do it! It is now Friday and he is going to leave on Sunday! I will have to say Jeanne does a fabulous job! She is able to get in touch with both of Eddie's brothers and their families; I am able to get my sister and her family. I also contacted both of my daughters and they have said they will be able to make the party on Saturday! Jeanne ordered a cake with a flag and all the decorations. We will have the party at Jeanne's house under the pretense that we are going over for dinner and to show the baby to Aunt Jeanne and Uncle Joe! Summer is so excited I just hope she can keep the secret long enough not to tip off her dad! If he finds out, he won't go. He is a pretty shy guy and he does not like being in the spotlight of anything. He has refused to let me schedule a going away party for him so this is the only way I am going to be able to do it so the family can say their goodbyes.

The night of the party has arrived and Thomas went to Traci's to pick up Kevin. He will meet us over at Jeanne's around seven. Eddie and I go ahead and go to Jeanne's so we will be in place with all the others when he gets there. I am so happy to see we have a full house. Everybody is here! Thomas is going to be so surprised! Everybody parked around back so Thomas will not suspect anything. When he arrives at the house, everybody hid behind all the furniture and Jeanne went to the door to let him in. As he enters through the foyer all of a sudden, "SURPRISE!" Everybody jumps out and I thought he was going to jump out of his skin! Then a big grin spread across his face as he scanned the room and saw all of his aunts, uncles and cousins! The chatter in the room rose to a level of enormous level and there was laughter throughout the room. I can not help but to sit and watch my son as he interacts with his family and see the carefree nature and happy young man that he is, knowing this is going to change as I know the nature of war and I know what is in store for him. *My heart is filled with joy but it is also filled with pain at the same time!*

Dad (Eddie) began snapping pictures. *He is the family photographer.* We began to take silly pictures, serious pictures and it is a great time. Our family has always been a close family and when you put us all together, it really becomes a party! We play darts, shoot pool, eat, and dance until late in the night. It is also the first time we have all five of our grandchildren together at once so we get pictures of that too!

As the night winds down, and it is time to say goodnight, that is when it becomes bittersweet. The night has been wonderful but now it has become serious as it sets in that this is going to be the last time many of the family members are going to see Thomas for a very long time. They will all wish him well, tell him to keep his head low, cheer him on, but in the back of everyone's mind is the question is: Will he come home? Will he be safe? As the party ends, there is a sadness and heaviness in the air…

The month of February slips by like it was flying and March is here before you know it. Thomas calls as often as he can and keeps me updated on everything that is happening. They are currently in process of getting all the prerequisite work of getting their affairs in order before they leave for Mississippi and their intensive desert training. They will be leaving directly to Afghanistan from Mississippi so these things have to be in order prior to their leaving for Mississippi. This includes getting their Wills, Power of Attorney's and bank accounts assigned to someone who can help them while they are away and assure their bills get paid if they are unable to do so. "Mom, can I put you as my Power of Attorney? And put you on my bank account? I need someone to help pay my bills and child support," he asks? "I am taking Traci off all my accounts and I am also putting you as beneficiary of my life insurance to make sure my kids are taken care of!" "I will be happy to help you son," I say. "You will have to leave me a copy of exactly what you want done and what you need to pay. I will make sure it is taken care of that way you don't need to worry about anything except your job!" *The part I didn't like was when I have to get a copy of his Will. This is really hard! No mother wants to have to see a Will for her child! It makes it all too real that there is a possibility he may not come home!*

Thomas does not have time to file for divorce now and his mind is not clear enough to think about that. He made it absolutely clear that everything was to go to his children and Traci is to get nothing. "I will file for divorce when I come home! I am not the one who wanted it this way anyway. This is her doing!" Anger flares in his voice. *Just talking about this enrages him so much. He needs to stay focused on his mission for now.*

CHAPTER 9

Saying Goodbye
Train-up / Mississippi

Saying Goodbye-
I have dreaded this day now for several months. We are headed down to the Eustis Armory for the final going away party for our young soldiers. They will be leaving for their three month "train up" in Mississippi and they will then deploy from there over to Afghanistan. They will not be allowed to come home after this train up so this is going to be goodbye! I can't believe this will be the last time I will see my son for more than a year. *Will I ever see him again? Stop! Stop thinking like this! This is the worry of a mother's heart and soul.* I have gotten him a Strippling Warrior necklace he has asked for. This is much like the cross or rosary for other religions. I have always called him my Strippling Warrior. The story of the Strippling Warriors is about two thousand young boys who were called to war to defend their homes when a large and fierce people was attacking them. They had never had any training or experience in such matters but they were righteous young men. They were taught in their youth by their mothers to rely on the Savior and to love their God. They faced an army of over ten thousand experienced, fierce, bloodthirsty warriors and when the battle was over, by remembering the teachings of their mothers, they defeated the army and not one life of the Strippling Warriors were lost. *Thomas is my Strippling Warrior!*

We will go to Tampa first and pick up our daughter Christy and her husband Brian and then to Lakeland to pick up Summer, our granddaughter;

Thomas' daughter. Thomas will need as much support as he can possibly have at this time. My cell phone rings, "mom? Are you still coming?" It was Thomas, again. "Of course we are son. Dad and I are on the road now. We will be in Tampa soon and then over to pick up Summer. We will be there in plenty of time before the dinner is supposed to start ok?" *He always gets so nervous! I don't think that is ever going to change!* "Ok…I was just checking," he says with a nervous little laugh. "Well, I'll let you get back to driving and I'll talk to you soon, I love you mom." "I love you too son."

We arrived in Tampa, where Christy and Brian live. They have already picked up Summer the day before so we will not have to make another trip over to Lakeland before heading to Eustis. We are all happy to see each other but there seems to be sadness in the air as well. It almost feels like a cloud of despair! Even Summer, who is now six years old (going on sixteen) has a sadness about her and she has always been a jolly child. But, Summer is a daddy's girl and she is very worried about her dad. She knows what is happening and she is somber today. "Nana, are we going now? I am ready to see my daddy!" I guess that is our clue! The ride will take approximately a hour and a half and everyone is a little nervous. Summer who is normally chatty is now melancholy and sits staring out the window in deep thought.

Eddie made good time on the road and as we drive up to the armory, Thomas is waiting out in the parking area waiting for us! He is dressed in his BDU's as are all the guys. He rushes over to the car and Summer jumps in his arms! "Daddy!" "Hey pumpkin! How are you?" there is a small tear in his eye as he hugs his daughter very tight. The rest of us exit the car and take turns getting our hugs! *He looks so handsome even in his BDU'S! I am so proud of him!* "Ya'll come on in and let me introduce you to the guys and to Sgt. Chadwick" he says. "There's lots of food and the other parents and family members are here too!" he says. He is trying so hard to be upbeat and happy. The guys are "pumped" and ready to go! We move from the parking lot into the main building of the armory and it is full of soldiers all dressed in BDU's. Family members are lingering close to their soldiers. Mothers are holding onto their sons arms, girlfriends are holding the hands of their lovers with tears in their eyes. Fathers are looking somber as if they know a secret that no one else knows but they stand tall with pride beside their sons. There are tables of food lining the walls of the building, with decorations hanging all around. This is supposed to be a party but the mood is not quite that jubilant.

We make our way to the food line, fix our plates and then we all find a place outside to sit to eat. Summer sits with her daddy, practically on his lap the whole time! Thomas and Brian head off around the compound so Thomas can show Brian all the Humvees and Tanks that are present. They finally return and Thomas takes us back inside to introduce us around. The first person we find is "Rob". SPC Larry Robinson is Thomas' best friend. "Hey Rob, I want you to meet my parents! Mom, Dad, this is Rob". We extend our hands to shake, "Nice to meet you Rob," I say. "Nice to meet you ma'am". He said. Next is SGT Chadwick, "Hey Sarg" Thomas says, "I want to introduce you to my parents". We exchanged our hellos and then as we talkf SGT Chadwick said, "I promise, I will take care of your boy ma'am, I will bring him home safe for you!" *Looking in his eyes I believe he will do it!*

The time is getting short. The buses will be here in less than an hour to pick up the guys to take them to Mississippi; from there they will go to Afghanistan. One more hour and I won't see my son again for over a year! There is sadness in my heart. It feels like a part of me is being ripped out. I am trying so hard not to cry and yet my eyes seem to tear up every time I think about it. Everyone is taking pictures, flashes are going off and it looks like strobe lights with all the flashes. The families are grouping off into separate areas inside and out to spend as much time as they can with the time that is left so they can have private time with their loved one.

The buses finally arrive and the time has come for us to say goodbye. I knew this was going to be hard but I don't think I was prepared for just how hard. Christy, Summer and I are crying. Eddie and Brian have somber countenances but they are trying to be upbeat and positive. Thomas is also trying to be strong but there are tears in his eyes as he kneels down to hug his daughter. "Daddy, I don't want you to go!" Summer cries. "Pumpkin, this is daddy's job, this is what I do. You have to be strong for me ok?" Summer throws her arms around her daddy's neck and cries. "Ok daddy, I will be strong." "I am going to miss you so much" she says. "I am going to miss you too pumpkin." I can no longer hold back my tears. This is the most heartbreaking scene I have ever witnessed. This little six-year-old girl is so much a daddy's girl and it is so sad for her to worry about her father and have to wonder if she will ever see him again. "Daddy, you are coming back aren't you?" she asks him. " I sure am pumpkin" He holds her tightly.

It was my turn. "Son, you do whatever it takes and you do whatever you have to do to come home, you understand?" "Yes ma'am." "I love you son, I am proud of you! Call me anytime you can!" "I love you too mom". I hold his face in my hands and looked into those beautiful baby blues. *For a short moment there was that connection, where no words were needed. My son, my buddy, my baby, I was going to miss him terribly!* We have bought him a laptop computer to send with him and set him up on Yahoo Messenger. "I will keep my computer on all the time." I say. "I will look for you! I don't care what time it is, if you get a chance to buzz me, I will be there ok?" "Ok mom, I will I promise!"

"Ok guys, time to load it up!" The Sarg was calling everybody to the bus. "I gotta go mom." One more hug for everybody all around and he hurried off. We watch as he loads up on the bus. The buses pull out and that's it. They are gone. We look around and all that's left are family members, mothers, fathers, girlfriends, brothers, and sisters all standing watching as the taillights of the buses disappear out of sight. You can hear light sniffles and crying in the night as the families disperse to their vehicles to leave. The moon is full and bright with so many stars shining in the sky as we enter our car to leave. I cannot control my tears and light sobbing. A light rain starts to fall as if the heavens are crying too. My heart feels like I have just lost a piece of it.

"He's only going to Mississippi for now mom" says my husband. "He still has a couple of months before he leaves for Afghanistan, so he won't be in any real danger right now." *This is his attempt to help console me. It doesn't really make me feel any better.* It was a long quiet ride home…

Train-up/ Mississippi

The arrival to Mississippi was a somber and exciting day for all the guys. Although the guys are nervous about their current call, they are also amped up and ready to go. These next three months are going to be nothing but extensive training to prepare them for battle in the desert. Thomas has promised to call when he can or email if he gets the opportunity. We are not sure what he will be allowed at this point. Much of the mission from this point forward will be classified and for the safety of the group they may or may not be allowed contact home. I am now on "Red Alert" so to speak. I am a bundle of nerves and wondering what is happening to my son! Eddie keeps telling me I am going to drive myself crazy. "Sheila, you have got to quit obsessing over this! There are other sons serving and going to war whose mother's do not act like this!" he says. "How do you know how other mother's feel or act?" I asked. *I can see right now this is going to be a long year between my sensitive feelings and Eddie's nature for logic!*

For Thomas, the first week seems to go slowly. They really don't have a lot to do. They are introduced to their housing and the rules. They are also assigned to their platoons. Thomas and the 53rd are attached to E Company Scouts and Snipers and will train with them. Thomas and Robinson team up as much as they can. They have become best friends and in this situation, you need someone you can depend on! It isn't long and vacation is over. The down time is over and it is time to get to work! It is grueling training that is going to take place. The first thing is to make sure they are in shape! At 0400 SGT Chadwick is in the barracks screaming at the top of his lungs! "Why are you sorry son of bitchs still in bed? Get your lazy asses up and out! You have five minutes!" Thomas jumps out bed and to the floor and begins to dress. He only *thought* boot camp was bad! The first day they are running doing push ups, pull ups, climbing the walls, side straddle hops and whatever the SGT can think of for them to do! This goes on from dawn to dusk. By the end of the day they are all so exhausted they can barely find the energy to take a shower. Most want to just lie in the rack and die! The guys on different days will instruct physical training. Today is Thomas' day. The Commander says, "I can take what ever you can dish out!" Thomas proceeds to conduct a strenuous physical training and the Commander ends up having to go to the med stop for a pulled hamstring in the middle of the training. Thomas just smiles and laughs to himself and to the Sgt's saying "he can't hang!" From that day forward when Thomas conducts PT the commander will not participate.

Thomas will ask him, "Sir, when are you going to attend my PT session?" the Commander will just reply, "**never!**"

The training is rigorous but the days pass slowly for me. Mother's day is approaching and I haven't heard from Thomas in several weeks. I go to work and keep my phone on constantly waiting for a phone call that doesn't come. I check my email constantly both at home and at work, looking for anything from Thomas. I keep my IM Messenger on day and night hoping Thomas will get a chance to use the computer and talk with me. *I don't know how mothers did it during the times when there was no technology available for communication and yet during these times when I hear nothing, I am pulling my hair out and crying at night wondering how my son is.* The thing is, he is only at training. How is it going to be when he actually leaves for Afghanistan? What am I going to do then? *Oh this mother's heart!*

On Mother's day I open my email and the first thing I see is an email from Thomas! This is the first contact I have had from him since he left two months ago! There was no writing just a picture…

I am so excited and all I can do is cry! The emotions are overwhelming and relieving just knowing he is safe and the fact that he took the time to remember me on Mother's Day; my sweet son!

This is the only contact I have from Thomas. For him training continues. They have another two months before they are to leave for Afghanistan. Their training is half way over. Every now and then I get a quick email telling me a little story about something funny that has happened or how tired they are. Occasionally he will just vent his frustrations but I am here to listen. I am so glad I can be here but sometimes I hear stories that will frighten a mother's heart! It doesn't matter how old your child is, they are still your children!

Today I received an email from Thomas. He tells me how they are bunking down in the tent using sandbags for pillows. Yesterday, he lies down after a long day of training and as he adjusts his sandbag he grabs what feels like a *snake*! The next thing you know he is facing a large copperhead face to face so he has to grab his machete while lying down and chop his head off before he is bitten! These are the things that will make a mother's heart just miss beats and take years off your life! Of course Thomas and the guys think it is funny! Me? I am about in heart failure! Many more emails like this and you might as well plan my funeral! If **I** make it through this deployment it will be a miracle!

Of course there are some light moments too. In between all the work, our boys find time to play jokes on one another and Thomas is the instigator in many of these. He has always been a clown and never misses an opportunity when it presents itself! On this particular day, he and another member of his group are sent over to the Commanders office to retrieve some paperwork. When they get to the office they find the private on duty sleeping behind the desk. Right behind the desk is the rival units flag and it is unprotected with the private sleeping! Now this is just too inviting for Thomas to pass up! "How can we do this without reveling our identity?" he asks. Very quietly they sneak over and remove the flag, Thomas wraps his shirt around his head, lights a lighter as if he is going to burn the flag and they take a picture! The picture is then left for the Commander to see! They sneak out quietly without waking the private! The next morning all hell breaks loose. The Commander has all the units out in formation demanding to know who the culprit is in the picture! Of course no one confesses to the crime! It is not until this book that the identity of the thief has been identified! Needless to say the private who fell asleep was "smoked" mercilessly! The moral of this story is NEVER fall asleep on duty!

The months passed quickly and July finally arrives. It is time for the unit to deploy. I receive a call and Thomas seems tired and melancholy. "Mom, we will be leaving out in a few days. I can't tell you exactly when for security reasons. I just want to tell you I love you and dad," he says. I can hear the nervousness and maybe even a little fear in his voice. *Be strong Sheila.* "Well son, we love you too and we are very proud of you!" I say. "Just remember, you do whatever it takes for you to come back home, do you understand me?" "Yes Ma'am," he says "No, I mean you do whatever, understand??" my voice was urgent! "Yes Ma'am." "Thomas, you call me or email or IM me whenever you can! I will keep the computer on! And my phone too, ok?" "Yes Ma'am," he says. His voice is flat and void. "Ok, mom, well my time is up, other guys need to use the phone. I love you mom." "I love you too son" The line goes dead. I am left listening to a dial tone. I don't know if I will hear from him again before he leaves for Afghanistan or after he gets there! All I can do is cry! …

CHAPTER 10

Deployment to Afghanistan /
A Year in Hell

July o5, 2005- Today is airplane day. Flight after flight, it's going to be long. I'm a little afraid. More fear of the unknown as well as the fear that this might be my last day alive in the states. I just want to make it home alive. But if this war requires my life, I will lay it down without hesitation. Never surrender. – Journal of SPC Thomas Watkins

The day has come to deploy! Everyone is ready and yet there is an anxiety among all of the guys! Regardless of what anyone says, when it comes right down to it, men have to face their mortality when they head to war. Some may or may not come back. As we look around at each other, will it be you, or him or will it be **me**? This is the time when family becomes more important than it has ever been before! Did I tell my wife I loved her enough? Did I show my parents how much I appreciated all they have done for me? Did I kiss my children before I left? Grown men cry and tears come but no one notices, no one looks it is a given among them all, a silent code…

At home, we the families don't know THE day they are leaving, all we know is it is soon. Is it today? Will it be tomorrow, was it yesterday? Where are they now? We need to do something constructive; something to keep ourselves busy and work is not enough. Some of the wives have small children at home and now they have to be mother and father as well as work a job and worry about their best friend, their lover. Some of us are mothers and fathers and worry about our children. I have decided to start a website for our unit. I have a friend of my father's who does website development who is willing to help us set up a website just for our guys! We will call it "Letters from Home!" We will dedicate it to our unit and we will be able to post family pictures, have individual albums for each of the soldiers and be able to chat securely with our soldiers. Jim Carr, that is our website developer, is a genius! We will post each soldiers birthday on there so we will not miss a birthday! We will also be able to post a care package list so our guys will be able to tell us what they need or want. Each person who sends out a care package can post when they send out a package and to whom it was sent. They can also post if it was sent for the whole unit or just to the individual! My two best friends, Sharon Corbitt and Cindy Townsend will send care packages to Thomas but we will include enough stuff to share for everyone! There are eighteen guys in our unit! *This will keep me busy and help keep me sane I hope during this time!* Eddie's job is to keep me sane! Thank goodness we work together!...

This will be the first trip out of the country for most of our guys. What a time for them to visit the world! And what a place to go! Their first stop is Kurdistan. When the plane finally lands, all of the guys are anxious, tired and scared. The environment is different than anything most of them have ever seen and the temperature is HOT! They file out of the plane, quickly and somberly but on high alert not knowing what to expect. They are escorted to a large hanger with rows of bunks; beds stacked two high and are instructed to put up their gear. They are going to be here for two days until their orders come in when they can finally go in country to Afghanistan. In the meantime, they are just trying to adjust to the change of scenery and the reality sets in. They are really here, in a foreign place, soldiers everywhere, Hadji is here too and they are the new guys! They are like wide-eyed children surveying the layout of the new environment and not knowing whom to trust. They realize they have to stick together more than ever and the alliances made in the weeks before during training will now be more important than ever!

I receive a phone call late in the afternoon and unexpectedly I hear my son's voice on the other end of the line! I can hardly believe the sound of his voice. He sounds so much older and tired. "Mom?" "Hey buddy!" I am so excited! "Mom, I only have two minutes, but I wanted to let you know we made it here and we're ok." He says. "Where are you?" I ask. "I can't say right now mom." We both laugh. "I kinda figured that," I say. "Are you ok? You sound really tired." "I am tired. It's been a long flight and it pretty much sucks here already." *Stay upbeat; don't let him hear you sound worried, I say to myself!* "Well hopefully once you get settled in it won't be too bad. I know it takes some getting used to!" We both laugh again! "You can say that again." He says. "Tell dad I love him ok mom? I gotta go now. There are only two phones here and the other guys are waiting so I need to let someone else use them. I love you mom." "I love you too son, very much! Don't forget that!" "Bye mom" The phone went dead. Just like that! One minute he was there and then he was gone! Barely a few words said! So much I wanted to ask, so much I wanted to say! I am relieved he is safe for now but I am worried still. It seems I don't know if I can be satisfied. So what do I do? I lay my head down on my desk and cry…

After two days in Kurdistan, the orders finally come, and the 53rd is moving in country to Kabul and to Camp Phoenix. A large C-130 arrives and the guys load up and again they are in the air and on their way into hostile territory! If they were worried before, it is nothing like the anxiety they are feeling now! First of all, traveling in a C-130 certainly is not a 747 passenger jet airliner. There is nothing comfortable about a cargo plane! Secondly, this really is the real thing. Everything they had trained for! Afghanistan, Hadji, Osama bin Ladin, the Taliban! This is it! They reached Kabul Airport and the plane landed with a hard THUD! Everyone let out a sigh, relief? Anxiety? Maybe a little of both! They were handed one magazine of ammunition and transported to Camp Phoenix where they will be until they receive their final orders on where they will be placed in Afghanistan. The group will split up; first section will stay in Kabul and second section will be pushed out to Forward Operating Bases or FOB's. Camp Phoenix at least had the comforts and luxuries of shops and places to eat. It is a small base and the tents are air-conditioned. The FOB's are going to be nothing like this! The guys decided they might as well enjoy the time here while they can because the next twelve months are going to be hell once they leave here! For now they enjoy the recreation areas, shoot pool and take advantage of the hot showers.

A week passed and the orders came down. Thomas, SGT Chadwick, SGT Jenkins, SPC Robinson and few others will be leaving for Camp Michael Spann up in Mazar-E-Sharif. This area of the country is desolate and approximately three hours away from Kabul. They will have to convoy by truck taking roads that are dangerous and patrolled by the enemy. They are given full combat load of ammo, load up with their gear and off they go! Anxiety runs high, nerves are worn thin and tempers are short. This is going to be a long and hair-raising trip. Everyone is just hoping they will make it there with no casualties! Heck, they are hoping they won't even have to fire their guns if the truth is known.

Arrival to Camp Michael Spann

Camp Micheal Spann is named after Captain Johnny Micheal Spann, a CIA Agent, and a US Marine Captain who was the first American casualty in the fight on terrorism in Afghanistan looking for Bin Ladin. He was killed during a riot that broke out while interrogating prisoners of the Taliban. He is considered an American Hero.

The convoy sets out across the country through terrain that is strange and ominous. The guys have a severe adrenaline rush pumping through their veins and are on high alert! *Is this the day I am going to die?* Thomas thinks, as the trucks roll across the mountains. Thomas sits as the gunner behind the fifty cal machine gun on top of the humvee. His job is a spotter, that is to look for IED's that may be planted along the roadside. *Will I get to see my children again? I have got to get my head back in the game! Push these thoughts out, think Thomas, think! Stay alert!* The convoy is instructed to keep the line tight and never let any cars or other vehicles infiltrate the convoy at all costs. Any vehicle that gets too close is ordered to move away from the trucks, if they do not move away voluntarily, they will be forced away. They are forced off the road, or if a fifty cal gun is pointed at them, they usually move! As they pass through the different towns, their vigilance becomes more intense! They begin to scan the rooftops for snipers; they watch every door for any suspicious person who may want to shoot them or any possible suicide bombers. They scan the roads for IED's. The trip is long and tedious but they finally make it to the FOB without any incidence.

Although they have made it to the FOB without any major incidence, and there ia a small sigh of relief, they are still on high alert. Their unit is assigned an interpreter and they are also introduced to the ANA troops that they will be helping to train and run missions with. There are so many adjustments these young men are going through in just a short period of time! So much to take in! *I am a soldier! I can do this!* Thomas thought.

They find their housing, which consists of a large tent, set up to house their group with not many amenities. There is no air conditioning and the temperature is topping out at nearly 125 F. The tent is lined with bunks and each soldier is assigned one. SGT Chadwick says, "Welcome home boys!" He will become the father figure for the next year of this group of men. The men settle in. They are briefed on what their responsibilities are going to be over the next year. They are told about the dangers of the land, such as Cobras and Camel Spiders! "Keep your sleeping bags zipped tight because the camel spiders will slip in while you are sleeping!" they are warned. *Camel Spiders? What the hell are Camel Spiders? That's just what I need to worry about! As if I don't have enough to worry about! This is going to be a long year! Mom told me to be careful what I asked for!*
Camel spiders are just that; large spiders that live on camels. But, they are very large and they are very aggressive. They will jump on you and they will chase you! Oh, they are also very poisonous! They are also very territorial. That means, we are moving into *their* territory!

I knew the unit was somewhere in the Middle East but I have not heard from Thomas since they landed the first day. I have been as nervous as a cat on a hot tin roof the last few days. I have slept very little and my computer has been on constantly and I sleep with it on my bed! My cell phone stays on and it also stays close to my side at all times. They are seven hours ahead of us in time so the middle of the night here is their morning. The middle of my day is their early evening. I never know what time I will hear from Thomas. Rob (Robinson) has become like an adopted son to me and calls me mama too. So I now have two boys over there that I worry about. I have adopted the whole unit but these two boys Thomas and Rob are **my** boys! I can't help but to worry, helpless, knowing they have headed into hostile territory and not knowing if they have made their destination. It has been almost two weeks now and I have had no word. Thomas is very good at letting me know when he is safe. But I have heard nothing. The waiting is excruciating. "I am sure he is safe Sheila" Eddie tells me. "He is busy and has a job to do! He will contact you when he gets a chance," my husband reassures me. *Here we go again a father's logic, which does absolutely nothing to ease my fears!* The days at work are long and I am distracted. The nights are longer and I cry myself to sleep, when I can sleep. Most of the time I just stare at the computer looking for any word on the IM.

Thomas' son Kevin was a newborn when he left. We promised Thomas when he left that we would make sure Kevin would know who his daddy is and teach Kevin about his father. True to our word we have gotten our sweet grandson every weekend since his birth. I have a picture of his daddy on my computer that stays on constantly. We have a web cam set up on the computer so when the time comes and we are able to establish contact with his daddy, we will be able to talk with Thomas and see him via the computer. We also keep a picture of Thomas on the table and we show Kevin his daddy's picture and tell him whom his daddy is. Kevin has learned to say daddy and he points to the picture. He will go to the computer and pat the computer and say "daddy?" It is so adorable. I think at this point he thinks the computer **is** his daddy! Damn this war! It breaks my heart! It isn't just me that is missing my son so much, but the children are missing their father! I know Summer is also devastated over the fact that her father is gone. She is older and much wiser. She knows the risks and she is suffering with ulcers at the age of six from worry that her father might die! Damn this war!

I am sitting at my desk at work when my phone goes off. I do not recognize the number. I am the conference coordinator for the USAF and I am always getting phone calls from contractors, DOD personnel and other customers in reference to the World Wide Review that is coming up. I answer the phone expecting it to be business related when I hear, "Hi mom!" For a second I pause and then I just squeal out "hey baby! How are you?!" "I'm good," he says. "So where are you, if you can tell me," and I laugh. "I'm in Mazar-E-Sharif," he says. "This is where we will be ..

All of a sudden I hear a scream and then the phone starts banging, "Thomas? Thomas?" still banging of the phone, scuffling around... I hear "holy shit!" my heart is racing a hundred and ten beats a minute! I have no idea what is going on and my imagination is going wild! "Thomas!" Finally Thomas is back on the phone, he is winded a little bit but he is laughing, "Damn camel spiders!" he says. "What?" *I hate spiders!* "All that over a spider?" " Mom, you don't understand, this is not a little spider, we are talking about a spider that is as big as my head!" *Holy shit!* "You have got to be kidding!" I say. "No mom, look em up. I'll send you a picture! These suckers are poisonous too!" "Well you can keep them!" I say! Now we are both laughing. "I saw that sucker coming over my stall and the whole line cleared out!" he said. "Yea I heard you screaming," I laughed. "Not just me!" he said. "Did you get it" "No! It got away!" "Oh crap now what?" I asked. "We'll get him later," "Well mom, I'm gonna have to get off here, my time is up! I'll try to catch you on the computer later! Tell dad I love him! I love you mom." "I love you to son!" I said. *I am so sad. There is never enough time on the phone!* " You stay safe ok?"

"Yes Ma'am" "love you mom, bye." The phone went dead. As usual, I am so happy to hear from him, but as soon as he hangs up, I lay my head on my desk and cry. *I miss his beautiful blue eyes. I miss my son!*

I send out a newsletter to all the family members and close friends letting everyone know I have finally heard from Thomas today! The response is overwhelmingly rapid in return. Everybody else in the family is just like me; praying and on pins and needles, hanging on the next time we will hear from him to make sure we know he is safe. It is amazing at how many lives just one-person touches in the whole scheme of things! I talk with Cindy today and we begin to work on the website to make sure we will have it up and running in the next week or two so we can start corresponding and coordinating the care packages now that the soldiers are in a stabilized location. The family readiness group is also waiting for the website to go online and set up their individual family albums. *Busy, busy, busy, that's how I deal with this situation! It makes me feel closer to my son! It makes me feel useful instead of sitting around and doing nothing and feeling helpless!*

Introduction *To War*
July22, 2005-
It has been a few weeks since the last time I have written in here. In these few weeks I have learned more than I ever imagined. I am now in Afghanistan. It is very hot here. It topped out at 123 F. today. When I first arrived here I was pretty nervous. That has all changed now. Now I am just alert and waiting for the next thing to pop off. A couple of days ago we spotted an IED. It was an artillery round. Thank God it did not detonate or a lot of us would be dead right now and saying we passed by it several times! To think, that would have been it right there! I would have not had the chance to watch my children grow or even tell my family how much I really love them. Even worse, I would not have told *a certain girl how I feel for her. Being here I realize just how short life really can be. One minute you're here and the next you're gone. There are a lot of graves on the side of the roads here. Most of them little.. When you die, they just bury you where you die. Children are the ones who often meet this fate! The child

mortality rate here is higher than I have ever seen. It saddens me and at the same time makes me angry! It makes me more determined than ever to eliminate these terrorist Mother F***** so that maybe one day this country can be just like the U.S. and a child's biggest fear will be bedtime and not will he or she die the next day! Every time I see the children, I can't help but to think about Summer and Kevin and Lil' A and if they were in that situation; I would want someone to help.

Most of the people here are very kind and they love us. It isn't what everyone back home thinks. They are no longer just Hadji. They are people with real faces and real emotions. In ways they are just like us. They strive for a better life. They live by their religion and they love their families.
I sat down with our interpreter and talked with him for a while. His name is Abdula and he is a native Afghanistani. He is twenty years of age and a very nice guy. He told me about his girlfriend and how he is working to save $10,000.00 American dollars in order to ask for her hand in marriage. He said he is very much in love with her and he wants to be with her forever. He asked me about my life in America and I told him. He then gave me a very long lecture of how I need to straighten up and quit committing sins against God. He said premarital sex, drinking, smoking and cursing I need to quit. I blew it off, but inside I knew he was right....
Journal SPC Thomas Watkins

The weather is so damn hot here and we stay in full battle rattle except when we are in the FOB. Since the tents are not air-conditioned it is impossible to stay cool! We don't have the same amenities that the guys down in Kabul in Camp Phoenix so supplies are limited. We are lucky if we even get mail or our so-called care packages in. The trucks take fire along the route in and out along the mail run and sometimes it is too dangerous to even go and get mail! We try to find things to keep us amused when we are not running missions or when we are on down time, which is few and far between! Today Rob and I caught two small camel spiders and put them in a coke bottle and watched them fight! That was pretty awesome! Those suckers are pretty wicked! We finally got our computers up, we didn't even have access to email or internet until recently. We all pitched in and bought a satellite so we could have computer access. This will help the morale of the men a lot. I will be able to talk to mom. That will make her feel better as she worries way too much! I will be able to talk to my son too! I am excited about that!

We are running several missions a day. So far they tell us we have run more missions than any other unit that has been assigned here. I know it keeps us tired. The insurgents and the Taliban are relentless. These people have absolutely no regard for life whatsoever! Occasionally we team up with one of the British units stationed close by and that's pretty cool. I have met some good guys who have become my brothers in this fight!

There are two routes we patrol on a regular basis. These routes cover a large area of territory and it seems we clear it out one day and the insurgents just return overnight. We clear out the IED's when we find them and have the bomb squad come in and explode them and before you know it, the some bitches come back and plant new ones! The engaged combat is what is scary as shit. Its one thing to hear about someone *might* shoot at you, it's another thing when you have some asshole shooting at you and you know he wants to kill you! The adrenaline goes wild and all you can think of is shoot like hell and get the hell out of there! I worry about my buddies too! So far we have not had any casualties and I thank God for that! I keep my Strippling Warrior on my dog tags that mom gave me for good luck and my handkerchief in my pocket! *I sure miss home!* Some of our humvees are armor plated but we still have soft-shelled vehicles so these are at great risk for these IED's and put our men in great jeopardy! Our next mission will be coming up soon and the tension is rising around camp. SGT Jenkins has gotten pretty cranky! His skin is not doing so well in this heat and he needs some meds for his face. I really need to make sure I ask mom the next time I talk to her to send some for him…

It's been a few days since I last heard from Thomas! I have been busy working on the conference and trying to keep busy. I sleep with the computer on and of course I am at the computer all day. I have the IM on and I watch constantly to see if his little Icon lights up! It's almost like that Icon mesmerizes me! My cell phone has become an additional limb to my body! I have become so tired these days. I stay up late at night watching that stupid little Icon just waiting to have a few minutes to talk with my son; any word to know he is safe and doing ok! Then it's up early again and back to work and having to take care of my responsibilities concerning my job! I am managing the Letters From Home website and watching to see if any of the guys post any special needs requests for the care package.

Cindy and Sharon have been so wonderful in making sure they have rotated their care packages to the troops. So far we have made sure they are getting some personal amenities such as deodorant, baby wipes to help cool them off and freshen them up, of course they want their cookies and believe it or not their favorite is the cheese gold fish! All the little things we take for granted here. *It's funny how the little things make them so happy and grateful.*

Eddie and I decide to work on a video to send to Thomas called Letters From Home. We use the song Letters From Home and Eddie actually sings the song, and we put it to a power point presentation with pictures from home. It is a quite touching video but we want our son to know exactly how proud we are of him and how much we miss and love him! We want him to know he is missed and there are people here at home that are supporting what he is doing! We want him to know that no matter what; we want him to come back home! The video takes a couple of weeks to finish, but when we finally get it done we send it to him on a disk he can keep and look at whenever he is missing home.,,,

Today has been another long day of missions. The guys are tired. I am tired! I have had little sleep. It seems like we finish one mission and we turn around and have to do another one. Our days our running together and we are working twenty-hour days at a time. Morale is low at times. It seems like we are forgotten down here. Sometimes we get mail, sometimes we don't, and it just depends on whether the trucks can make it through. It has been awhile since we have gotten any packages but mom says they have sent several. We have yet to see them!..

AUG 5, 2005
Another entry into the journal. Not too much new. Tomorrow we leave on a four-day mission to Sheberghan, Pola Comrie and Maymana. We will be traveling through some pretty rough areas. The threat level is high and all of our adrenalin is pumping full throttle. I don't care what happens as long as we all live. I don't too much mind getting into shit with small arms; AK47's and such, but the RPG'S scare me shitless. Maybe it's cause I know it's one hit and it's game over! I had another dream about a *certain girl last night. I don't know what's wrong with me. I can't seem to get her out of my head no matter how hard I try. I catch myself thinking about her often. I have to quit thinking of that if I want to come home alive! I need

to keep my head in the game. But still I keep coming back to this! Even knowing she doesn't want me or love me that way. Maybe its just cause I'm here. I just can't slip and let her know how I feel or I could screw up the friendship we have built.

JOURNAL SPC. THOMAS WATKINS...

The mission we are about to embark on is going to be an all day trip. Although Sheberghan is only eighty miles away, the terrain is rough and filled with IED's and hostiles. We load up in humvees and start out around 0400. As we pass through some of the smaller towns along the way, we stop at a bread store to buy some bread. Our interpreter immediately comes back out of the store and reports to SGT Jenkins "there are three Taliban soldiers in the store!" SGT Jenkins immediately goes to the Major and passes along the information. Since the Taliban Soldiers are unarmed and not showing any aggression toward any of the U.S. or ANA Soldiers, the Major orders everyone to stand down! *What the hell? I thought! What the hell are we here for?* These are the orders we have. Engage only if engaged upon. *I'll just have to get those bastards later!* We load back up and move out. Not one of us are happy about leaving the Taliban Soldiers behind but, another day! After four days, we return home to our FOB without any major incidents on this particular mission. As I always say, any day above ground is a good day! We are exhausted. We clean up the trucks and head for the sack! I'll try to talk to mom when I get up! She is going to be worried but I have got to get some shuteye! ...

It's only been a month since Thomas has been in Afghanistan but it seems like forever! He sounds so tired every time I talk to him! He sounds so different. His happy, joking sweet nature has been replaced with a depressed, flat affect. He no longer jokes much and when he does it is a very morbid almost revengeful attitude. I worry about what is happening to my son. I worry about his physical and mental well-being. This war is going to take a toll on so many people! I see it in the wives and mothers I talk to on the IM and emails. Already it is taking a toll on the mothers left behind with small children but everyone is standing strong. We have eleven more months to go! Heaven help us! God help us and that is exactly what it is going to take! A lot of prayers, a lot of faith and strength to keep a good attitude to help boost the morale of our soldiers when we talk with them! Never let them know we are worried, never let them hear us cry! ...

Most of the missions up to this point have been fairly benign. In November we start taking fire on our missions and the adrenalin of all us pump thorough our veins like a rushing river. Today we traveled on a route through one of the towns we usually patrol on a regular basis and all of a sudden out of nowhere we started taking fire from an AK47. We cannot pin point the location of the shooter and the population of civilians was too dense to begin fire. We decide to blow through town and try to escape the fire without casualties to preserve the lives of the civilians and our group as well. Luckily we are able to move without any causality to our troops. Once we return back at the FOB we inspect the trucks for any damage and the nerves of the guys are on edge and intense. Our next mission is scheduled for the next day and we are not going to get much sleep
tonight! …

I don't hear from Thomas everyday and that can be so nerve wracking for me! Everyday at work I am distracted watching the IM just waiting to see if his little Icon lights up. I don't want to leave for lunch just in case I might miss his message! Every time my phone rings I am hoping it will be a call from my son! Work goes on and life goes on! Today is Friday and I always look forward to Fridays because Eddie and I go and pick up Lil man (Kevin) and keep him for the weekend. He is growing so big and it is so much fun watching him as he grows. He is so much like his daddy when he was small. He looks just like him and has the same personality. He is soft hearted and gentle and he is a happy baby. *And those same blue eyes! When he looks at me with those eyes, I see the same connection, I see his daddy! I see my son in those eyes. Something about those beautiful blue eyes!*
I pick him up today after work and as we go through the door his eyes just light up when he sees his papa. "Pawwwpaw" he says and reaches out for him! Just then he spots the computer I keep up with his daddy's picture on it and he looks at it and says, "daddy?" "Yep," I say, that's your daddy! I mean the picture but I am sure he thinks the computer is his daddy! He has never seen his daddy except on the computer. And the only time he has ever talked to his daddy is on the computer! All weekend he will walk over to the computer and he will either pat it or lay his head on it and say, "daddy." It is cute but it is also heartbreaking. *Will he ever get to see his daddy? I have to push the thought from my mind!* "Have you heard from Thomas today?" Eddie asks. "No, I haven't heard from him in a few days. I think he is out running missions. I know he will call or IM when he gets in, he usually does so I won't worry," I say. I can see the worry on Eddie's

face. He never says a lot and never shows too much emotion but I can tell he is worried about his son. He knows I hear from Thomas frequently if not almost daily so if I haven't heard from him, he worries too! He doesn't say anything else. He begins to play with the baby. "I'm putting together a care package to send to the guys, can you think of anything particular you think I should send?" I ask. "Send lots of chocolate candy," he says. We both laugh. "I'm serious! Men love candy and you know they can't get it there. Not to mention it will be a nice treat to remind them of home!" he says. I was thinking more like practical needs! Leave it to a man to think of food! But he had a point. So, chocolate candy went on the list! I watched Kevin and Papa play and think back a few years when Thomas and his dad used to play. *I miss my son…*

The Suicide Bomber

We have been running at least two missions a day sometimes more. Our days are long and most of us are sleep deprived. We are constantly on alert and we drink a lot of the Red Bull just to help us stay awake sometimes. I have been assigned to run special missions with the ETT (Embedded Tactical Training) guys. My usual job is the gunner on the Humvee. My duty is that of the spotter. I look for IED's and I sit behind the 50 cal machine gun and I look for snipers. Today is no different. We are running a patrol traveling through the city of Mazr-E-Sharif. As we approach the city we begin to notice the crowd is acting funny and we suspect we are either going to hit an IED or run into an ambush. Our convoy slows down and the crowd begins to disperse quite rapidly. I begin to vigilantly scan the rooftops for snipers. All of a sudden I am thrown violently forward and my head smashes into the gun. My ears are ringing and for a second or two I am very disoriented. I hear my SGT. screaming in my headphones "we're hit! Look for snipers!" I am still trying to collect my thoughts and I am trying to figure out if **I** am hit. I can barely hear because of the ringing in my ears and I almost start firing at everything that moves! Our convoy begins to speed out of town! About that time we receive orders to turn around and go back and investigate the situation! My ears are still ringing. When we get back to the square, we begin dispersing the crowd and that is when I notice I have blood and body flesh all over me! We find a suicide bomber who has detonated a bomb and is blown apart all over the ground. Part of his body is on my humvee and on the humvee behind mine. Half of his body is up in a tree. Some of the ANA soldiers traveling with us find his head laying in tact a few yards away. His eyes are open and when I look at those eyes it's like they are looking at me! *I realize at this very moment how close I have come to death. The bomber detonated his bomb a little too soon. If he had been a few paces closer I would be gone instead of just having been hit by the blast! Outside you show no fear; you show no weakness. Inside you want to cry. War is not what it is cracked up to be! I miss home. I miss my children. I miss my family…*

We load back up and the convoy continues on our mission back to the FOB. We clean the trucks and I head for my tent. I call mom. I need to let her know I am back from my mission and ok so she won't worry and to be honest, I just need to hear somebody from home! …

It is another normal day at work and I am swamped! I spoke with Thomas earlier today on the IM just to say good morning but he was leaving out on a mission. I never know where he is going only that he is leaving. Always in the back of my mind I am worried when I know he is gone, but he is always gone. He said he would let me know when he gets back. As usual I continue to watch that little Icon as if mesmerize by it. I am busy answering emails and phone calls related to the World Wide Review when my cell phone rings. I look at the number but I don't recognize the number. "Hello?" "Mom?" I hear on the line. "Thomas?" I say" "Hey mom." I hear. "Thomas? Are you ok?" I ask. "Yea, I'm ok." He says. His voice is flat and void. *Something is terribly wrong!* "Thomas, are you sure you are ok? You're not hurt are you?" "No ma'am. I just wanted to let you know I was ok and I love you." He says. " I love you too son. Did everything go ok on your mission?" "Yea it was ok." He says. Again his voice is flat and void. He doesn't sound like himself. "Mom, I am supposed to get leave to come home for Christmas. I am not sure when that is but I know it will be in the next few weeks. I will let you know ok?" "That will be wonderful! *I am really excited now.* "Mom, I just want to get out of here. I need to come home!" he says. "Well when you come home for Christmas that will give you a break. How long will you have?" I ask. "If I get to come it will be for two weeks, but not everybody gets to go. So don't get your hopes up." Again his voice is flat. "Son, are you sure you are ok?" "Yea, I'm just tired, I'm gonna have to go now mom, I just wanted to let you know I was ok. I love you mom. Make sure Kevin knows I love him and tell Dad I love him too Ok?" "I will, I promise" "Ok, well I gotta go. I love you mom" "Thomas, make sure you say your prayers ok? Heavenly Father will help you get through this ok?" I tell him. "I will." He says. The line goes dead.

I don't know what is wrong, but a mother's intuition knows that something is very wrong. I don't know what has happened but something has. Did he have to kill somebody today? Did he almost get killed today? Did one of his friends die today? Whatever happened on his mission today has definitely affected him and he is dealing with something that is weighing very heavy on his heart. I could hear it in his voice. I can tell by the way he was talking. A mother knows her son! I will have to pray extra hard for him. *I can't stop the tears as I cry for my son…*

Christmas was just ten days away and we still don't know if Thomas is going to get to come home, but we continue to decorate the house as usual and we buy his gifts and plan on him being home! Becky and Summer make plans to drive up from Florida but we will wait and see when he will get his leave, so they can be here when Thomas is home and Summer can see her daddy! We all pray very hard that he will be one of the soldiers that will get the pass to come home! I am very sure he will get a pass! I just have faith that Heavenly Father knows he needs the time home! Two days later I get a call, "Mom?" "Hey!, How are you?" "I'm just great!" he says. "I got my pass! I will be home for Christmas if everything goes right!" he says. "I'm supposed to be home by Christmas Eve! Do you think you and dad can pick me up at the armory in Eustis?" *I am so excited I can hardly keep from jumping up and down!* "Of course we can! What do you think?" I say. "Well, I'll call you when we are almost there so you will know when to come ok?" "That will be fine! I am so excited! I will be so excited to see you son! I miss you so much! I love you!" "Me too mom, it will be good to be home." He says. "Tell dad I love him ok?" "I will." I said. "Well I gotta go, I just wanted to let you know." "I love you mom" "I love you too son!" "Bye mom." The line goes dead. Our conversations are always so short and abrupt! But he is coming home for Christmas! I immediately get on the phone and call Eddie! I can't wait to let him know that our son is coming home!

Christmas Leave
The time is growing closer and the family is getting more excited! Everybody keeps asking when Thomas is going to be home! So many people want to come and see him! All the Aunts, Uncles and Cousins! Jeanne is having the family get together at her house as usual so everybody will get a chance to see him then. I am not sure how Thomas is going to react to that though. He has already expressed that he does not want a lot of people around. He

doesn't know Becky and Summer is going to be here yet. I want this to be a surprise. He is looking forward to seeing Kevin!

Thomas calls to let me know he is actually going to be in Eustis the day before Christmas Eve. "Mom, do you think you can bring Kevin with you?" "No, we can't get him until Christmas Day." I tell him. "Ok." He sounds so deflated. He has no idea that Becky, Summer and Alana (Becky' youngest daughter) will be with us! The day before Christmas Eve we are on our way to Eustis when I get a call, "Mom?" "Hey!" I say. "What time do you think you will be there?" "How far are you from the armory ?" I ask. "We are about a hour and a half away." "Well we will be there waiting on you." I say. "Ok mom, I can't wait to see you! I love you Mom. You sure your gonna be there?" "Yes son, we will be there! And I love you too! Dad says Love Ya Mean It!" We both laugh. "Tell him Love Ya Mean It!" he says. That's a phrase our family uses to each other. We arrive at the armory and there are other families there waiting for their soldiers to arrive on the bus that is coming in. We are all so excited that we are going to see our soldiers as it has been over nine months since we have last seen them! There is much apprehension as to what to expect. We have heard in their voices over the phone the changes that have taken place, especially for the first time soldiers. *I know Thomas sounds so different than he did before he left so I am not sure what to expect when he gets off that bus!* Some of the more experienced wives try to give us advice, like just don't push them, and don't ask them too many questions. They are going to act strange just being back in normal society and may be jumpy at little things. I don't care about any of that! I will just be happy to see my son!

We are so excited as we see the bus coming around the corner and pulling into the armory! I am about the jump out of my skin and I can hardly contain Summer! "Nana, Nana! Is my daddy on there?" she squeals. "Yes honey, he is on there" Now she is jumping up and down! It seems like forever but the bus finally pulls up to the front of the armory and the men starts filing out. As soon as Summer sees her daddy I can not hold her back, she goes running as fast as she can. "Daddy, daddy!" As soon as Thomas sees her he drops all his gear and the biggest smile comes across his face as he kneels down and receives his daughter in his arms. For a long minute they just hold each other in a long embrace and I cannot hold the tears from streaming down my face. It is so heartwarming. Finally he is able to pry her arms from around his neck and pick his gear back up. She holds onto his leg the whole way over to where we are standing. I throw my arms around his neck and give him a big kiss. "Hi mom!" he says. Next his dad first reaches out to shake his hand and then he pulls him to him and gives him a long hug. "I've missed you son." He says. "I've missed you too dad." Thomas says with a small tear in his eye. Becky then steps out of the car. I thought I heard a small gasp. "Heeey!" he says. Then for a long moment they embrace. Becky has tears in her eyes. She is speechless. We all get in the car, other than Summer, it is actually a quiet ride home.

Once we get home it seems like everyone is fighting to help Thomas with his bag. He finally says, "I can get it!" We all just laugh and let go. "Can I get you anything to drink or eat son?" "No ma'am I'm good" "Are you sure?" I ask. "Mom, I'm good." He now sounds a little agitated. "Ok." I say. "I'm just really tired mom, it's been a long flight and I need some rest. I didn't mean to snap at you." "Actually I understand son, dad gets like that when he travels!" I laugh. " I have the room out in the garage area set up so you, Becky and the kids can stay. If you want me to keep the kids in here tonight I will." "No, I want them with us." He says. "Ok, well dad and I are going to bed. Do you want to have family prayer with us?" "Sure." He says. We proceed to have family prayer and Eddie and I go to bed.

Today is Christmas Eve! I think this is probably the best Christmas I have ever had. At least the one I have actually been aware of just what Christmas is all about. I am so thankful that I am going to have my entire children home. Christy and Brian are driving up from Florida to see Thomas and to be home for Christmas. Tori and the girls will be here too! We are also going to have Kevin but Thomas doesn't know that yet! The girls are up early as their parents sleep. *Thomas is not really Alana' dad but her father died before she was born. Thomas was with Becky when Alana was born and has always been around when she needed somebody to help. That is Thomas' gentle heart. He has always had a gentle heart! Lala he calls her.* We decide to make cookies. I set the girls up on chairs at the table as I begin to cook the cookies. We are going to make my grandmother's chocolate oatmeal cookie recipe. The girls will have to roll them in powdered sugar balls. That is always so much fun! *Quite messy but fun!* I have always loved making these cookies when my children were small and now I get to pass it down to my grandchildren! Just as I start putting the chocolate balls on the wax paper for the girls to roll Christy and Brian walk in the door! Of course they come in the back door, which comes through the garage room, and wake Thomas and Becky! I can hear the laughter and chatting from the kitchen! I continue to work on the cookies with the children. Eventually Christy makes her way into the kitchen "Hey woman!" she says. "I was wondering if you were ever going to come in and speak to your mother!" I say! We both laugh. "Aunt Chrissy!" Summer bolts from her chair with powdered sugar all over her hands and runs to Christy to give her a hug! Without a thought Christy gives her a big hug, then looks at her hands and says, "Ewwww, what is on your hands?" "Sugar!" she says indignantly! "We are making Christmas cookies!" "So I see. Are you getting any of the sugar on the cookies?" "Yes!" Christy laughs and goes to the sink to wash the sugar off of her. She then comes over and gives me a kiss on the cheek, "Hi mom" she says. While we chat she sticks her hands in the cookies and starts rolling. Summer looks at her and says, "You know how to make these cookies?" "Yep, I used to make these cookies when I was your age!" "Is that right Nana?" "Yes ma'am, she has been making them a long time!" "Oh." They all continued to make cookies until they are done.

Thomas and Becky finally come in the kitchen as we are wrapping up the cookie mess. Both children go running to their parents! By this time Dad has joined the party so to speak and Brian too. The kitchen is getting full! "Good morning mom." Thomas says as he hugs me. "Good morning! Did you sleep well?" He smiles at me and says, "I did! It sure is nice to have a nice bed to sleep on for a change!" He then winks at Becky. She turns three colors of red as she slaps him. "Mom I need to do some Christmas shopping. I haven't had a chance to do any. I was wondering if you could watch Summer and Lala for a little while?" "Yes, I don't see that as a problem. And then as most mother's do I had to add, "don't spend all your money on gifts, we don't need a lot of gifts, just having you home is a gift!" "Mom! I want to buy things! I don't know if I will ever get a chance to buy things for people again! And I want to get my children some things!" he said. I let it go. I then say "I do need to tell you though; we are supposed to go to Aunt Jeanne's tonight like we always do. So you need to make sure you pick up a gift for the round robin gift." I saw him turn a little pale. "Who all is going to be there?" "Just the family. Our family, Aunt Jeanne and Uncle Joe and Uncle David and his family." "Mom, I don't know if I can handle all those people right now." "Well, Becky will be there to help you and if it gets too bad you can always go outside to get away, do you think you can try? They all really want to see you while you are home!" "I'll try mom." *He still doesn't know we are going to have Kevin and he has never seen Kevin except once right after he was born! I think it will be different when he sees Kevin. He will want to show Kevin to the family!*

I am hoping we will be able to have Kevin at the house before he gets back from shopping. I want to see the reunion between father and son. Kevin has only seen his dad on the computer. He has only seen his picture so I am hoping he will recognize his daddy when he sees him in person. I know Thomas will recognize Kevin because we have been sending pictures as he has been growing and he has been seeing him on web cam and talking to him on web cam. As soon as Thomas left to go shopping, Eddie left to go pick up Kevin and I stayed home to watch the girls. Christy and I visit and start to cook a ham to take over to Jeanne's later that night. Brian goes with Dad. Becky goes with Thomas.

Dad and Brian pull into the drive and Summer is so excited. She can't wait to see her brother. She runs to the door to meet them as they come in. Kevin runs to her arms. "Is this my sister?" he asked? "Yes, this is your sister!" We have been telling him for several weeks that his sister was coming to see him. Kevin is much smarter than his ten months of age. He speaks like a two year old. But Eddie and I have been working with him quite a bit with his language. He gives her a big hug. He looks at me and says, "I love my sister!" "I know you do" "Awww," says Summer. *They both have such large hearts just like their father!* Lala comes out the door and he looks at her. "Who is that?" he asks. "That is Alana, she is my sister." Says Summer. "Is she my sister too?" asks Kevin, with a puzzled look on his face. "No honey, you and Summer have the same daddy, Summer and Alana have the same mother." "Oh like me and Chelsea have the same mother but not the same daddy!" he said. "You are so smart! That is exactly right!" "Ok, but can I call her my sister?" "Sure if you want to!" Summer and I looked at each other and smile. He runs to Alana and tries to give her a hug. Of course Alana didn't want a hug and pushes him away. "Nana, she won't hug me." He looks at me with sad blue eyes. *Those big blue eyes full of hurt.* "Well honey, she will need to get to know you first ok?" "Ok nana" His feelings were hurt, but he tries very hard not to let it show.

Papa was sitting on the couch watching all of this. Kevin runs over to the couch and of course he has to relay all of this again to him. Papa can make it all better. After a little talk Kevin feels better. He then spotted the computer sitting on the stool that has his daddy's picture on it. He leans his head on the computer and begins to pat the computer. "Daddy" he says. Somehow this brings him comfort. All of a sudden the back door opens and his daddy walks through the door. Kevin looks at who is coming through the door. He looks at the man coming through the door. He looks at the picture on the computer and then the man in the door. "Daddy? He says to the man coming through the door. Then he looks at the computer. Daddy? He says again. Then he looks again at the man coming through the door, Daddy? And he looks at me confused." "Yes honey that is your daddy! He is back from the Army and he is here to see YOU!" He takes off running toward his daddy. I can see the tears in Thomas's eyes at the fact that his son recognizes him! He picks him up and they hug each other. "Daddy you are back from the Army?" Thomas laughs, "Yes I am back from the Army!" Kevin then looks at the computer again. He was still trying to figure out how his daddy got out of the computer! That was his next question. "How did you get out of the puter?" Everybody in the room laughed. Now Kevin wanted down. He thought he had said something wrong. He came running to me and I had to explain he had not said anything wrong!

Thomas brings in his packages from his shopping and he and Becky take them to the back bedroom to wrap them. Christy and I have finished cooking the ham and the girls and I have finished the cookies. It is almost time to get ready to go to Jeanne's. I am so thrilled for so many reasons! Christy talked to Tori earlier and she and Jason and the girls are going to be at Jeanne' also, so I am sure I am going to have my whole family together tonight! What better gift could a mother ask for? *Still lingering in the back of my mind however, is the fact that Thomas is going to have to go back to that hellhole. I can see the haunted look in his eyes. Although he is trying to be happy there is something that is not quite right. A mother knows her son. I have not had a chance to talk with him. But I will.*

We load everything up in the car and head to Jeanne's. There is a chatter of happiness and excitement in the air. We look at all the Christmas lights along the way with a few oooohs and aaahhhs from the children along the way. Once we reach Jeanne's house we unload the car with all the presents and take them in and put them under the tree. We are the first ones there, which is actually good for Thomas so he is not overloaded with a load of people bombarding him all at one time! Jeanne and Joe are so happy to see him and Jeanne is squealing with joy! Thomas who is usually very warmhearted, is a little standoffish and seems a little uncomfortable when hugged. I noticed this right away. *Again he has that dead far away look in his eyes! This is not my same son that left here ten months ago and I feel a twinge of sadness in my heart. He is hurting inside, a hurt even a mother can't heal.* The other guests begin to arrive and of course they all can't wait to see Thomas! Every now and then I would see a genuine smile from Thomas as he hugs the cousins. He loves the girls. Tori came and he was genuinely happy to see her. He loves his sisters! And hugs the nieces, he loves his nieces! That's when I see the old Thomas shine through. That's when it is good to see him! Surprisingly he does really well during the night as we mingle and shoot pool and chatter and mingle as a family. He looks really happy tonight! It is good to see him happy as he plays with his children and watches them open their Christmas gifts! We are a goofy family. We take goofy pictures and act goofy as we always do! The night ends too soon and it is time to go home. The children are tired. The old folks (like me) are tired. We all say our goodbyes and goodnights. Everyone hugs Thomas again and wish him well. I notice he is a little less inhibited than he was when he first came in and that is good to see. He is a little more like Thomas. Family is what he needs. I believe Family heals everything! Love is what he needs!

We have to take Kevin back to his mother's because she wants to have him home for Christmas Day. We drop everyone home and papa and I take Kevin back to his house. This saddened Thomas but unfortunately there is nothing we can do. We make plans with Kevin's mom to get Kevin the day after Christmas so Thomas can spend a little more time with him before he has to leave. Even though she and Thomas are still legally married, she is living with another man and is pregnant with her boyfriend's child. She and Thomas obviously are not on speaking terms to say the least! Thomas has refused to give her a divorce until he returns home stating he just can't deal with the stress of haggling out the details and trying to stay focused on his mission. So he has just blocked it from his mind for the time being. That is the reason Becky decided to come and stay. She and Thomas never married when they had Summer but they have always been friends and they have always loved each other. *I know Thomas would marry Becky but she has always for whatever reason backed out. I know she loves Thomas but I don't know why she treats him like she does. But she is good for him now.* Becky, Summer and Lala are going to stay a few more days but are going to go back to Florida by New Years.

Since Thomas is going to have to leave out of Eustis, he has decided to go back to Florida with them and stay with Becky until he has to leave. They seem to be getting along very well and I am hopeful that maybe this time it might finally work out between the two of them. Eddie warns me again, not to get my hopes up. "Sheila, mark my words, she is up to something. Once she gets to Florida, she will dump him again." He says. "I can't believe she will do that Eddie. They have been getting along so well! Thomas has spent so much money on her for Christmas! He is going down there for New Year's. They are going to spend New Year's together!" "Just mark my words, I love Becky, you know that, but she is up to something." He says. "He is so excited, that will kill him!" I say emphatically. *Now I am worried about my son, how can I talk him out of going? I know he won't listen to me! I have got to try but I know him, he is going to follow his heart and it is going to get broken again!*

Christmas morning arrives and it is almost like old times in the house. Dad and I lay in bed as we listen to the chatter of the children in the other room. This time is isn't us, but Becky and Thomas that is awakened at the break of dawn to see what Santa brought! Oh the revenge of being grandparents! We can even hear Christy and Brian mixed in the voices. "Daddy look!" says Summer. "Mommy, mommy!" screams Alana trying to get louder than her sister! "Look Aunt Chrissy, Aunt Chrissy!" "I see!" says Christy trying not to be grumpy. Dad and I just lay behind our door laughing as we listen. "Do you think we ought to go out there?" I ask. "Are you kidding?" We both just laugh as we get up and retrieve our robes. "Are you ready?" He just gives me the "dad" look. I laugh and we head out the door to the living room. "Nana, nana, papa, papa!" Summer came running with her toys in hand to show us what Santa brought! Thomas and Becky both look as if a bus has run over them. Dad and I just grin at them. "It sure is fun being the parents on Christmas isn't it?" I say with a little sarcasm. "Up at the crack of dawn and all." As I head to the kitchen for a glass of coke. If looks could kill I think I would be double dead! "Mom, you're just not right!" Christy says. Then she starts laughing. Now she gets the death stares! The kids are running around like they are hyped up on a double sugar overload! Papa takes his glass of coke and heads to the den! Out of sight, out of mind!

I finally find a time when Thomas is alone and he and I walk out to our favorite spot in the backyard and sit on the swing like we used to do and begin to talk. "Son, I know it has been difficult for you the last couple of days since you have been home. I have noticed how uncomfortable you have been." "Mom, I'm afraid to get comfortable or to let myself start to feel anything because I know I have to go back. Over there you can't feel anything. If you feel it will get you killed." *I was at a sudden loss for words and my heart was stung with a horrible pain.* "I know you have to stay focused over there and it is hard to turn your feelings on and off, but don't let it harden you too much," I tell him. He glares at me with a look I have never seen from him before. "You have to be hard mom! You don't know what it is like over there. Those people have absolutely no regard for life! It's kill or be killed! I don't even belong here anymore!," he says. I had no idea what to say to my son. We both just sat swinging. "Thomas, do you have to go to Florida? Can't you stay here a little longer and let dad and me take you back when it's time for you to go? We would really like to spend more time with you!" "Mom, I already told you I am going to Florida! I am going to spend New Year's with Becky, no disrespect to you and Dad, but I want to have a little fun before I go back! I am going to go out and party a little." We both laugh. *I knew I would not be able to change his mind. I knew what he had in mind. He is a partier and he wants to be with Becky. Unfortunately, I, like dad, believe she will break his heart again and I don't know what that is going to do to him right before he has to go back to that hellhole!*

It seems like the week has flown by way too quickly! Christy and Brian left a couple of days ago and now Thomas and the girls are packing up and preparing to leave for Florida. Tomorrow is New Year's Eve. Thomas will have to report back to Eustis in just a few days and I will not get to see him again before he leaves so this is my goodbye until he comes home for good. I didn't think it would hit me this hard! I knew this was just a leave! *I just want to grab him and hold him and tell him he just can't go back!* The mood in the house all morning has been quiet and somber even though we started it out with family prayer as usual. I have quietly but continuously wiped the tears from eyes. I am trying not to make this hard on Thomas but I am dying inside myself! When Eddie is nervous or trying to lighten a mood he sings. He has been whistling and humming all morning but he has been very hyper! He has offered his help to pack up all the gifts. He has been playing with the kids outside. When everything is done and they are ready to go Becky and the girls come in first and tell us bye and hugs all around. Thomas comes in last. "Well mom, I guess it's time," he says. His head is slightly lowered and his eyes are slightly red as if he has been crying. "I want you to drive carefully ok?" "I will" "Thomas, I love you son. I am going to miss you very much. Please, do whatever you have to do to come home ok?" "I will mom," he looks up at me tears now in his eyes. "I love you mom!" There is a long embrace and it was like I was holding my small son in my arms again. I didn't want to let him go! I wanted to shelter him from all harm. My heart is breaking, all over again! "I don't think I can do this goodbye thing too many times," I say. We both start laughing! "Dad, I love ya man!" "I love you too son! And I am with your mom, do whatever it takes to bring your butt back home!" Father and son hug for several seconds. Thomas turned almost too square, and headed out the door. The girls are in the car waiting. Dad and I walk outside to watch them drive off down the road, waving the whole time. *It looks like a Hallmark movie, nice family driving off, grandparents waving goodbye. Everyone lives happily ever after. I go inside and sob myself to sleep…*

The drive is long when you factor in two chattering children and the constant "are we there yet?" But we finally make it safely to Becky's house without incident. I call mom so she won't be worried. Sue (Becky's mom) greets us and throws her arms around my neck. I still haven't become comfortable with people hugging me yet and I don't want to feel! I hug her anyway. After taking all the toys and luggage inside we sit and talk for a while. *Everybody wants to talk about what it's like over there! I don't!* I finally change the subject and Becky and I get Sue to agree to watch the girls tomorrow night so we can go to a New Year's Eve party! Now we're talking! After bathes, we all hit the sack for the night!

The morning comes early with the kids up at the break of dawn! I am usually up anyway! *Last night I was up and I was a little panicked because I couldn't find my weapon! It took me a few minutes to realize I was on leave!* We spend the day trying to get ready for the evening. Becky has to get her hair done and her nails and all those things women want to do to make themselves beautiful. *I thought she was beautiful anyway. I have always wondered why it takes them all day long to get ready for an event!* **Finally** it is time to go! We head over to her cousin's house where the party is being held! The music is jamming and I finally get me a beer! I have been waiting all day! People start filing in, friends I haven't seen in quite some time! Becky and I are together; life is good! I move over to the bar to speak to an old friend and when I come back into the living room I see Becky's old boyfriend, John. The problem is he isn't alone, Becky is with him sitting under a blanket on the couch and they are very cozy together. I can just stare for a minute. I don't feel anything. *I am not too surprised; dad warned me this was going to happen, dad was right, he is always right.* I just look at both of them as I head for the door. I am going to go call some friends, get drunk and get laid! I am successful in all three!...

Some Gave All...

Leave is over and it seems like it has taken a month just to get back to the hellhole. I can't believe I am back here. Christmas leave seems like a dream now. Maybe it was. The action has kicked up to high gear just in the two weeks since I have been gone! It's been two weeks since I've been back here now. I have been talking with mom when I can on the IM and that is the only thing that keeps me sane sometimes. I'm worried about her a little. Every time I talk to her she seems to have a doctor's appointment. She says she's fine. She seems fine…

Thomas has been gone now for two weeks. He's back in that hellhole! That's what we call it! The hellhole! He told me what happened with Becky on New Year's. He seems ok but I know he is hurting over it! I can feel it! He won't let himself feel it though. I have another doctor's appointment today to get the results of my lab tests. They have tested me for Cystic Fibrosis of all things! I have been having problems for quite a while but lately I have been having problems with my lungs. After having several tests and ruling things out they have decided to do a sweat test. I have already been diagnosed with Fibromyalgia and I am now in quite a lot of pain. I don't dare let Thomas know I am sick and I have made his sisters promise not to tell him anything until he comes home! *I do not need him worrying about me! He has enough to worry about and I need him safe!* Eddie is out of the country on business today so my sister Cathy is going with me for this appointment. I already know the results however. The advantage of being a nurse, I know how to go around the system. I have gone to the hospital and picked up a copy of my records and the results are positive. I won't let the doc know I already know. I am not sure I will tell the girls right away either. I need to process these results and see what the plan is. Basically since there is no cure, I already know all we can do is treat the symptoms. At least it explains why I feel so tired and I have problems breathing!

I didn't go to work today but luckily my job has been very accommodating and they let me work from home when I am ill. I see Thomas' little Icon pop up! "Hi mom!" "Hey there buddy! What's up?" "Not too much! Just checking in before I leave on my mission. How'd the doctor appointment go?" "It went fine! Just went for lab results, nothing to worry about! (Smile) "Ok, well, I'll check in when I get back ok? I gotta go! Love ya mom!" "I love you too son! Be safe ok?" "I will! Bye mom." He was gone! This how it was. Short little blurbs. But at least I hear from him. He is such a good son. He is so good about letting me know when he's leaving and when he gets back! At least I know where he is. Well somewhat. I don't know what his missions are and I always worry every time he leaves, but I guess you can't have it both ways. Either I don't hear from him and know nothing and worry or I know he's leaving and worry. Some times I don't know which is worse! *Yes I do! I am glad I know when he is leaving. At least I somewhat know where he is and I know when to expect him back. He is so thoughtful to let me know when he gets back! That mother son bond!* I've said it before but I will say it again, I don't know how the mothers in the past did it before the technology we have today! I don't think I could take not hearing from my son for months at a time! *I think we both keep each other somewhat sane through this bloody tour!*

Today is just another day in the hellhole. That's what mom and I call it! We are off on another short mission today. I am traveling with JCF British Army, trailed by three Group SF. We have stopped to observe a game of hiscotchi. This is a game like a polo game but they use a dead goat that the locals play. The game is pretty interesting to watch and it is a little entertainment for us! It is time however for us to load back up and head back toward town. I am in the lead humvee. I am the gunner. I am also the spotter for IED's for the convoy. My job is to spot any IED's hidden on the sides of the road that Hadji has set up for our demise! I am good at this job. It's getting late so we have decided to take a shortcut we know back to town. All of a sudden a very loud explosion startles me! *What the hell?* I hear kaos in my radio and we realize it is not our vehicle that is hit! I turn around in the turret and realize the soft skin British humvee trailing behind us has been hit! We stop our vehicle and jump out and run to render assistance. As we reach the vehicle I realize it has been hit by a remote detonated IED! *How the hell did I miss it? What have I done?* The scene is chaotic, body parts and blood is everywhere! Two men are barely still alive one is dead. I immediately grab the soldier in the drivers seat and pull him from the vehicle. *Time has slowed to a crawling pace. This can't be real!* This soldier has a piece of shrapnel lodged in the left side of his head and his left leg and arm are ripped up pretty bad! I begin to attempt frantically to stop the bleeding and keep him sustained until the medics arrive! I look over at the second man. My buddies are trying to start and IV on him! He is in even worse condition! *If that is possible!* We load them into a vehicle and the medics rush them to the British Medical Center. We are left here at the scene. Now it all seems surreal. I feel like I am going to be sick! *That should be me! I missed the IED! THAT SHOULD BE ME!* We let the back up team clean up the mess and the convoy, we continue on our mission and back to the FOB. The radio is quiet for the ride home. I find out that the driver was pronounce DOA and didn't make it! *It's my fault; these were my friends, it should have been me...*

CHAPTER 11

The Homecoming

The last few months have been really bad! I only have three weeks left in this hellhole then I'm outta here! It seems like I have been here forever in hell. *Even though I want to go home, I am a little afraid because I don't know if I will fit back into that environment!* Little by little I am starting to ship some of my stuff to my mom. I do everything I can, not to think about how much time is left or it will drive me crazy! It's just work and sleep when you can. We won't know exactly what day we will be leaving anyway and they won't give us a date. The date keeps changing every time they tell us one thing, then they come back and tell us it has been extended. I will believe it when it happens! …

I am getting so excited! I can't believe July is finally here! Thomas will be coming home this month or so he says! The frustrating thing is every time we get an approximate date they change the date! I keep checking with the family readiness representative who is actually the SGT's wife but she can't give us any information either. We can't post anything on the Letters from Home website due to security reasons because they do not want anyone to know when the troops will be moving in or out! Even though the website is secure there is always a chance that someone, including the enemy, might hack it! We have had to be very careful what we post on the website all along! Mostly we have just posted little notes to our guys letting them know we love them, or pictures of the kids. We have birthday reminders so we could send birthday notes to all the guys to let them know they were not forgotten! All this now seems like it has been so long ago and I can't believe eighteen months have passed! What seemed to have dragged on forever is now drawing to an end! I can feel a sense of closure coming but at the same time there is a great sense of apprehension. So many times it is right at the end of the tour that something happens and the soldier doesn't make it home! *Stop thinking like that!* It brings to mind my Great Uncle who was on his last mission in WWII and then he would be coming home. He was a fighter pilot. All he had to do was finish this last mission! He was shot down on that last mission and was killed! *This is NOT going to happen to your son!* The phone rings..

"Hello?" "Hi mom." "Hey buddy! I was just thinking about you!" I say with my most cheerful voice. "Are you getting excited about coming home?" I ask? "Not really. I will get excited when I am on the plane home. They keep changing the date so much!" he says. I laugh, trying to keep the conversation light. "Well, I am getting excited! I can't wait to see you! Have they said anything else about a new date yet?" "No, and I couldn't tell you if they did. I told you we couldn't tell you. The family readiness coordinator will let you know." He says a little irritated. "Oh yea, I forgot. You know how dingy your mom is!" I say, trying to lighten his spirits. "Are you ok today?" "Yes ma'am, I am just a little tired, I just got off a mission, haven't eaten yet or had a shower. I just wanted to call and let you know I was ok and tell you I love you." *He sounds so depressed! Especially for someone who is about to come home!* "Thomas, promise me you will be very careful these next few weeks ok? I don't want you to get careless or complacent! I know you will be coming home and I want you to stay alert ok?" "Yes ma'am" "Are you sure you are ok?" "Mom, I am nervous about coming home. I don't know if I will fit in anymore!" he says. *He sounds so depressed and sad. My heart aches.* "Son, you will do just fine. Just remember your prayers! Heavenly Father will help you ok?" "I don't know if God will still love me mom and I don't want to talk about it!" *I was flabbergasted!* "God always loves you son, trust me!" "I love you mom, just pray for me ok? I know you have pull with him. I gotta go get some chow and shower now ok?" "Ok" "Tell dad I love him, mean it. Bye mom." Before I could even say goodbye he was gone. I have never heard my son sound like this before! Why would he say such a thing? Something is really bothering him, but what? I know he has been complaining of headaches over the last few months and has been treated for them off and on at the dispensary. All I can do now is really pray hard for him!

Over the past few months I have heard more and more anger in his voice when we talked. Even in his IM messages, the tone showed a lot of anger. It didn't take much to make him angry. I found more and more I had to take great care about what I say or he would fly off the handle. He and I have always been very close, we have been close even throughout this whole tour of duty and he has always told me everything that was bothering him, but lately he seems to be falling further and further away from me. I will see his little Icon on and try to talk with him and he ignores my call. I leave him messages on his Yahoo and sometimes it takes him a couple of days to return my messages. *This is so unlike my son!* I have even had conversations with Eddie about it. I am extremely concerned because I know in my heart something is very, very wrong, but I don't know what, and he won't talk to me. It is the first time in all of his life that he won't talk to me about what is going on in his life! He will be home in a few weeks! I have to keep thinking about that! I am exuberantly happy and will continue to focus on his homecoming. I have already sent off for a banner to post on the house that says "WELCOME HOME SPC. WATKINS." We are going to hang it on the front of the house. I have flown my flag everyday since he left in the front yard on a large flagpole I made my husband put up right after he was deployed! We have kept yellow ribbons on all of our trees and the mailbox during his absence. I want him to know that we have missed him and how proud of him we are! *I still can't get the words out of my mind "I don't know if God will still love me."*...

Time is passing so slowly! Day after day it's the same shit! We go on mission after mission and no sleep. Then when I do go to sleep the nightmares come. I can't let the others know I am having nightmares because that will show weakness! I can't get that British Humvee out of my mind. *I killed them!* I see the head of that suicide bomber looking at me! I am a killing machine and all I want to do is kill something or somebody! Is this how I am going to be when I go home? *I don't belong there anymore! This is where I belong!* I want to go home, I want to see my family. I don't want to stay here, but maybe this is where I need to stay! I haven't told mom yet but I am already looking at signing up with some mercenaries so I can come back. They make good money and my time in the guard will be up soon! I am a soldier! This is what I do! Maybe I will just get out! I don't want to do this anymore! *Who is going to hire a killer back home?* ...

I continued to check with the family readiness coordinator to see if she had any news on when our guys are going to come in. I did find out they will be coming into Ft. Stewart Georgia and not Eustis when they do come in. We still do not have a date but it will be within the next couple of weeks! Eddie and I are excited they are coming into Ft. Stewart because that is much closer to us. We will not have to drive so far to pick him up and drive home! Erin, Thomas' friend from childhood has been seeing Rob for the last year, (Thomas introduced them via web cam!) and is coming up from Florida and will be riding over with us! She will be meeting Rob face to face for the first time. She is so nervous! We are making welcome home posters to take with us! I am making shirts that have pictures of Thomas on them that our family can wear showing our soldier welcoming him home! Erin of course is making a shirt for Rob! I want to plan a big welcome home party for Thomas for the family since everyone is so excited and can't wait to see him! They all want to welcome him home too! All this time I am still working and this is one of the busiest times of the year for me as I am right in the middle of planning for the World Wide Review and registration is in full swing! I am so stressed out that it is taking a toll on my health and I am so tired! I will take a few days off when Thomas comes home to spend with him! The time is growing closer! I watch my little Icon every day and hope Thomas will ping me. He doesn't always answer my pings anymore. *I still worry about his comment!* Today I see his Icon light up! I take a chance and ping him! "Hey mom" Hey! You're there!" "Yea, we just got back" he says. "How are you?" "Tired. Gotta go back out in just a little while." "Well that sucks!" I say. "Keeps us busy." "Well, it won't be too much longer now, and then you will be coming home!" "Mom, I don't want any kind of party or a bunch of people around ok?" he says. *I am a little disappointed.* "I kinda wanted to give you a welcome home party with just the family. Aunt Jeanne, Aunt Shannon, Aunt Cathy and their families, they all want to see you." " NO!" He says emphatically! "I just want to come home and have some time to myself! I don't mean no disrespect, but I need some time to myself and I don't want to see anybody ok? I don't want a party!" he says this again rather sternly. Although my feelings are hurt I agree not to have anyone there. "Ok, I promise." I say. "Thank you." He says. His tone was much lighter. "I just want to see you and dad and have a little quiet time. I don't think I can be around a bunch of people right now." "Ok." I say again. *My spider senses are really tingling now. Something is very wrong! I don't know what, but something is terribly wrong! This is not like Thomas!* I have to try and explain to all the family that we are not going to have a welcome home party right now as Thomas has asked not to have a lot of people waiting for him. He does not want a party when he returns. The family is disappointed but they seem to understand. I have promised to have a family get together once he has been home for a little while and has gotten reaclamated to his surroundings. "Eddie, why do you think Thomas is so adamant about not wanting to have a welcome home party?" I ask. "Sheila, you have to understand, he has been in an environment that is so different from this one. When I came back, I didn't want to be around a lot of people either. I didn't want to answer questions about what I was doing and you have to understand where he has been and what he has been doing. He has got to get used to being back into a normal society without being bombarded with a lot of questions." "I guess I can understand that." I say. *I am just so happy he is coming home! …*

They have finally given us our date! Two days and a wake up! That's how we count it! I'm outta here in three days! I still have missions to run! I don't want to get careless! I have to keep my head in the game! It's hard not to get short-timer's syndrome! But short-timer's syndrome will get you killed! We have two missions to run today! I will call mom on the IM when I get back! They are giving us the easy stuff or trying to but you still have to be on your toes. We were driving not too long ago around one of the mountains on these roads and SGT Jenkins flipped over in one of the fuel tankers. I just knew for sure he was a goner! Scared the shit out of me! I ran down to pull him out but he got out. We both were crying. He is one of my best buddies I have been with through this whole tour! We haven't lost anybody in our direct unit and I hope we don't! *Don't think about the British guys now!* We have run more missions than anybody else has ever run since they have been here without any direct casualties! I want it to stay that way. *Two days and a wake up and we are outta here!*

"Hey mom!" "Hey buddy!" I am so excited to hear from him! Even if it is on the IM! " Whatcha doing?" " Working, lol. What are you doing?" "Just got back from a mission." "How'd it go?" "It went fine. Nothing big, No problems. Kind of quiet." He says. "Just two days and a wake up!" I say. "Yes ma'am!" "Are you getting excited yet?" "Kinda." "Well I am!" I say. "Mom, what are people going to think of me?" "What do you mean son? Everyone is very proud of you!" "What about when they know what I've done!" "Thomas, they don't need to know what you've done! You have been at war! You have done what you have needed to do to get home! War is war; there are different rules for war! People are proud of you for serving this country! It takes a special person to do what you have done and people realize that! Do you understand that?" "Yes ma'am. Well I gotta go mom. I will talk to you soon. Are you and dad gonna be there to pick me up?" "Of course we are! You don't think I would miss that do you?!" "Ok." "Well, I love you mom. Tell dad, love ya mean it." He was gone! ...

The day is finally here! I am so excited I can hardly contain myself! Erin is here too. She too is so excited and quite nervous. I told her she would be fine. I know Rob. He is a great guy. They have been seeing each other for a year over the computer and web cam and they seem good for each other. Everything will be ok. We are all so excited to see Thomas. Thomas is like her brother. We all put on our shirts and get our posters. Eddie just shook his head. "You girls are so silly" he said. And I knew the next sentence coming "I never had anybody making such a fuss over me!" *If I hear that one more time I am going to kick him!* He just smiles at me because he knows it irritates me! We have a three-hour drive to Ft. Stewart so we load everything in the car and prepare to leave. The guys are supposed to be in sometime around five pm but family is supposed to be there by four so we can go through a briefing so we know where we are supposed to wait for our returning soldiers and know what to expect when they return. We will have to get a hotel again because our soldiers will not be released immediately as they will have to go through a debriefing first. I want to get there earlier so we can get a hotel before we go over to the base. The ride seems so long to me because I am such an impatient person. Erin follows us in her car so she and Rob can ride back to Florida together! We communicate via walkie talkie and we are both so nervous. Eddie on the other hand is cool as a cucumber and just sings and whistles and tells us to just settle down. *Easy for him to say! Sometimes I think he is so cold! But the truth is he is just a very logical person and does not work off of emotions...*

We finally reach Ft. Stewart and find a hotel! We get checked in! We get a room for us and a room for Erin and Rob. Rob's father is there also and we meet him for the first time. After getting our rooms we head over to the base to get ready for the plane to arrive with our soldiers, our loved ones that we haven't seen in such a long time! The crowd is full of parents, spouses, sisters, brothers, children and all kinds of family, holding banners, flags and wearing shirts with their soldiers and loved ones pictures! You can feel the excitement in the crowd! You can see the smiles, tears, and joy of those waiting for that plane bringing in the 53rd brigade! We wait and wait. Then the General gets on the microphone and announces that the plane is running late! *Par for the course! That is always Melvin luck!* He says it is delayed approximately forty-five minutes. You can hear the groan of the crowd! What can we do? Not a bloody thing! We have to just sit and wait! As if we aren't tense enough the General has just added more tension to our nerves. *Why is the plane late? Is it having trouble? Is there something wrong with the plane? STOP IT SHEILA!* I have flown many times and know the plane can run into bad weather and it will delay your plane. But I also know where they are coming from. *Did they have problems getting off of the runway? Did they take on enemy fire? Obviously our soldiers are ok; they are in the air because they are running late! That means they got out of the country! I am a nervous wreck! I can't wait to see my son, hold him in my arms!*

FINALLY, we see the double doors open at the end of the auditorium and we hear the plane as lands and the buses pull up to the back doors. After what seems like an enormous amount of time, we eventually see our soldiers start to file into the auditorium in a single line and fall into place in front of us on the auditorium floor. The grand stands erupt into an inaudible roar of clapping and whistling and whooping for our soldiers. We of course are all trying to get a peek at where our soldier is in line! Thomas is right up front! The soldiers have a stern and sober look on their faces as they stare forward. They do not look around and they do not look at the crowd, however every now and then you will see their eyes scanning the audience. Thomas finally scouted us out and you can see a small little smile on his face as it relaxes just a bit! We wave, hoop and holler like we have no manners at all! Jumping up and down. I have tears in my eyes as I look at my son who appears to be way under weight! The General of course has to give his little speech before he will release the soldiers to the families. When he finally does, you can hear the thundering roar of the bleachers as the families make their way off the bleachers and down to the floor to their soldier! The reunions are heart wrenching. As I make my way to Thomas, I wrap my arms around him so tightly that I think I will squeeze him to death! He hugs me but his hug is not what I expect. He gives me a quick little hug and then pushes me back some. "Hey mom." "Hi Son! I am so glad you are finally home! I can't believe you are really here!" I say with tears in my eyes! Before I can say any more his dad has made it over to where we are standing. They shake hands and hug briefly. "Hi son, how are you?" " Good, glad to be home." Thomas says, but there is no emotion in his voice. I am a little surprised at his emotion or lack of it. He just seems like a robot. I expect him to be more excited about being home and he is just, just…cold. All of a sudden I see SGT. Chadwick walking towards me. I turn to greet him. He offers his hand but I reach up and hug his neck, "Thank you so much!" I say. "I brought him home ma'am, just like I said." "Yes sir you did! And I am so grateful to you SGT! Welcome home! And THANK YOU again!" "It was nothing Ma'am." He then introduced me to his wife. After a few niceties, they went along their way. *I was so grateful to him and would be forever!*

"So what's next?" I ask. Thomas tells us we have to go out to the lawn and pick up his luggage they are unloading from the plane. So out to the lawn we head. Of course it is dark and they have just unloaded all the luggage for everybody out on the lawn all in one big area so you have to just pick through and try to find yours! The whole Brigade's luggage is on the lawn! *Boy is this a fiasco!* Everybody is running around checking tags, with flashlights and trying to find their luggage, and by the way, it has started to RAIN! What a mess this is! After about an hour we finally find all of Thomas' luggage and bags and put them in the vehicle. Next we have to fight the crowd of cars to get off the base! Thomas is going to have a one night pass off base and then has to report back on base tomorrow for his debriefing. All we care about is getting to the hotel, drying off and getting into some dry clothes. We are all hungry and tired! Thank goodness for good old KFC! We pick up a bucket on the way to the hotel and by the time we get there we are fighting to see who gets to take a shower first, I win! *Thank goodness I am a girl and my guys are gentlemen!*

Morning arrives early and we take Thomas back over to the base for his debriefing. We are unsure of how long this is going to take. Erin is spending the time with Rob's dad. They have to see a psychiatrist for their outtake as well so we are given an approximate time to meet them back at the office to pick them up. Eddie and I just ride around and tour the base since we have a base sticker on our car and check out Ft. Stewart since we have not been here before. We have already checked out of the hotel so when Thomas is finished with his outtake we will be ready to head home! *Finally! I can't wait! I will have my son home!* Thomas was at last done with all of his official business and ready to head home! We loaded up in the

Envoy and headed back to Warner Robins! The ride home was rather quiet. On several occasions I tried to start a conversation with Thomas but he was busy looking out the windows. He was in deep thought and his eyes were scanning, scanning. "Son, what are you doing?" All of a sudden he looked at me somewhat embarrassed, "I was looking for snipers and IED's," and he laughed. "Guess I have to get used to being back home." "It's ok, It'll take some time to adjust." I said. *He was sweating profusely.* "Are you OK?" I asked. "Yea, I'm ok mom." Dad had some snide remark to say and we both start to laugh.

The ride home takes forever it seems especially for Thomas because he keeps "looking for snipers and IED's" and he is quite nervous anytime a car gets close to ours. When I ask him why all he says is "We just never knew when a car bomber was going to blow up close to the convoy." We finally make it to the house; unload all of our bags and get Thomas settled back into his room. I am so excited to have my son back home! Finally this damn war is over for him! *Or is it? ...*

Sheila studied Journalism and creative writing at Polk Community College in Winter Haven Florida before switching her major to nursing. She has written poetry and song lyrics for guitar for the last thirty years. When her son was deployed to Afghanistan she helped develop and managed a website (Letters from Home) so the soldiers could have a way to communicate with their families while deployed. She and her husband produced a video "Letters From Home" where her husband sang and dedicated to their son while he was deployed.

Sheila was in constant contact with her son during his deployment through computer and phone nearly on a daily basis and helped to comfort him in some of his most distressing times. This was a very stressful time for both mother and son, but it also was comforting to both to know that they were there for each other. Mother was able to know that her son was safe after each misson, and son was able to vent and find comfort to destress with someone from home. This book will take you through that journey and show you the bonding of mother and son; a bond that was developed from birth and continued and strenghted through this very stressful time with the help of their very stong faith in the Savior. This is part one of a two part story. This will cover her son's life from birth through his return from Afghanistan. But that was not the end. Because as we know sometimes War Follows You Home!

Sheila is married with three children, Thomas being her youngest chiled and only son. She has five grandchildren. Sheila became ill and suffers from Cystic fibrosis, fibromyalgia, protein C deficency and seizures. She had to leave her nursing job and was working for the USAF with a government contractor as a Conferance Coordinator during her son's deployment. She became permanetly disabled from Seizures in March of 2010 and decided to write this biography of her son. She lives iin Georgia with her husband of 22 years.